Daily Conversations
with

God

Prayers for Women

Our mission is to publish and distribute inspirational products offering exceptional value and biblical encouragement to the masses.

Daily Conversations
with
God

Prayers for Women

DAY 1

Come Closer, Beloved

*In him and through faith
in him we may approach God
with freedom and confidence.*
EPHESIANS 3:12 NIV

Dear Lord, You are the God of the universe, and yet You ask me to come closer. I can't stand in Your presence, yet You ask me to approach with freedom and confidence. It's all because of Jesus, Lord, that I can do this! I praise You for the great gift of Your Son, who allows me this access to You, my Creator. I am so small, but I long to know You better. I am so weak, but I know You have power to spare. Help me to come to You again and again. In Jesus' precious name, amen.

In Your Presence This Day

"If my people, who are called by my name,
will humble themselves and pray and seek
my face and turn from their wicked ways,
then will I hear from heaven."

2 Chronicles 7:14 NIV

Dear Father, I thank You that Your ear is always listening for the cries of Your people. You are always listening for my voice, and You know it out of billions of others. My words are not just spoken to the empty air, but You give them Your attention. Forgive me for my sins today, Lord, for they are many. I rest under Your mercy.

DAY 3

Everything Is Possible

Abba, Father, all things
are possible unto thee.
MARK 14:36 KJV

How amazing, Lord—my Father is the Creator of the universe! Your infinite creativity formed the beauty of the earth and the intricacies of life. I know I can rest assured in Your strength, in Your might, in Your abilities. There's nothing on heaven or on earth that You can't handle. Forgive me when I try to take things into my own hands. Since You made the world and everything in it, I know You can take care of my small life!

Joint Heirs with Christ

*For ye have not received the spirit of bondage
again to fear; but ye have received the Spirit of
adoption, whereby we cry, Abba, Father. The Spirit
itself beareth witness with our spirit, that we are
the children of God: and if children, then heirs;
heirs of God, and joint-heirs with Christ.*
ROMANS 8:15–17 KJV

Thank You, Lord, for adopting me into Your family,
for making me Your heir, just as Jesus is. There's
nothing I can do to deserve this favor or this
acceptance. Your grace is all-sufficient. I now call
Jesus my brother, and together we share in Your
amazing glory!

Receiving Jesus

*But as many as received him, to them
gave he power to become the sons of God,
even to them that believe on his name.*
JOHN 1:12 KJV

Lord, I believe in Your name. Help me every day to believe still more. Take away the doubts and insecurities that the world shouts at me every day. Keep my eyes firmly focused on You, even when troubles come. Keep my ears attuned to Your voice, especially when I am tempted to listen to other voices. I welcome You into my heart—to make a home there now and forever.

The One Who Is

Who is like the LORD our God, who dwells on high?
PSALM 113:5 NKJV

Heavenly Father, today I'm grateful for all You are—the God who is, the God of the living, the great I Am. Your character is unchanging. You are the epitome of perfect holiness and love. Because of who and all You are, I believe and trust in You. Your truthfulness is indisputable and Your power is established. Not just for the majestic works by Your hand but for the pure glory of Your nature—I worship You today. Amen.

Grace for Everything

But he gives us more grace.
JAMES 4:6 NIV

Father, I'm thankful for Your *grace*—Your unmerited favor to me through Jesus Christ and that special strength You give Your children in times of need, trial, and temptation. If not for Your grace, I wouldn't even be able to approach You. Thank You for extending favor to me: forgiving my sins and adopting me into Your family. And thank You so much for that extra dose of perseverance that You keep giving to me in tough situations. I'm so thankful Your resource center will never experience a shortage. I praise You today for grace. Amen.

DAY 8

The Lord Almighty

*And [I] will be a Father unto you, and ye shall be
my sons and daughters, saith the Lord Almighty.*
2 CORINTHIANS 6:18 KJV

You, God, can do all things, for You are almighty,
all-powerful. Because You are my Father, I know I
can trust You to handle each and every aspect of my
life. Show me new ways that I can rely on You to
work in a mighty way in my life. I trust You with my
past, my present, and my future. You are God, and I
am not—and I am thankful that's the way it is.

Arise and Go

The word which came to Jeremiah from the LORD,
saying: "Arise and go down to the potter's house,
and there I will cause you to hear My words."
JEREMIAH 18:1–2 NKJV

So many times, Lord, I feel the urge to drop to my knees and pray. Yet I don't. Embarrassment, busyness, a dirty floor—they can all stop me from heeding Your call. Yet I praise You that You keep calling my name again and again. Please help me to trust You enough to stop what I am doing when I hear Your call. I am on my knees now, my King. I am listening to Your voice.

The Living Fossil

You are an epistle of Christ. . .written not with ink but by the Spirit of the living God, not on tablets of stone but on tablets of flesh, that is, of the heart.

2 CORINTHIANS 3:3 NKJV

Lord, You have preserved Your Word for thousands of years. It is uncorrupted, it is unchanged, it has not been forgotten. Like an animal buried and hammered into rock by time and pressure, it has come down to us, yet it is not fossilized: it lives! You chiseled Your law into rock for Moses, but now Your Word is written in our hearts. And we, too, will live uncorrupted and unforgotten but, thanks be to You, *changed*. Amen.

Luther, Wesley, Crosby, Etc.

Let the word of Christ dwell in you richly in all wisdom; teaching and admonishing one another in psalms and hymns and spiritual songs, singing with grace in your hearts to the Lord.

COLOSSIANS 3:16 KJV

Dear God, I don't know where I'd be tonight without the great hymns of the faith that have resounded in my head since I was a girl. Thank You for that legacy of music and poetry and for what You have taught me through meditating on those lines. I praise You for the men and women who penned the lyrics and music that still minister to Christians today. Thank You for the hymns that kept my heart tuned to You, even when I thought I was running far away. Great is thy faithfulness! Amen.

A Father's Mercy

I will be his father, and he shall be my son:
and I will not take my mercy away from him.
1 CHRONICLES 17:13 KJV

Thank You, Lord, that You will never take Your mercy away from me. No matter how many times I let You down, I can always count on You to pick me back up. I cannot understand this gift, but I am thankful for it, Father. Please show me ways to extend mercy to others in my life—especially to those whom the world may deem as "unlovable." Because the truth is, God, I know that most days I, too, am unlovable.

In the Inner Room

*"But you, when you pray, go into your inner room,
close your door and pray to your Father who is in
secret, and your Father who sees what is done in
secret will reward you."*

MATTHEW 6:6 NASB

Dear God, You know how often I pray and how
often I *don't*. You know that sometimes I use it as
a weapon. "Lord, give me patience!" I say in the
presence of those who are vexing me. Please forgive
me. That is not prayer. And Lord, forgive me for *not*
praying. Forgive me for wasting the quiet moments
that You give me with things that will be forgotten
in eternity. I want to know You now, *here*, even
before I am with You forever. Amen.

DAY 14

Getting to Know You

We loved you so much, we were delighted
to share with you not only the gospel
of God but our lives as well.
1 Thessalonians 2:8 niv

Dear Lord, thank You for reminding me today to pray for the people who witnessed to me before I was a believer. I was so ignorant of Your ways, Lord, that I didn't even know that was what they were doing! I thought they were just telling me about their lives, that we were getting to know each other, when really they were introducing me to their Savior. I praise You for how real You were to them and for their example of how sharing our faith is more about *conversation* than conversion. Bless those brave evangelists, Lord, and continue to do Your work through them. Amen.

God of All Comfort

*Blessed be God. . .the Father of mercies,
and the God of all comfort.*
2 Corinthians 1:3 kjv

You comfort me, Father, when my heart aches. When everything in my life seems to be going wrong. . .when the world is full of violence and disaster. . .when loss is everywhere I look. . .when hope is dying inside me, Your comfort never fails. Thank You for offering me that constant care in my life. Help me to always extend comfort, care, and compassion to others as well—ultimately leading them to You.

DAY 16

I Will Hear

"Before they call I will answer;
while they are still speaking I will hear."
ISAIAH 65:24 NIV

Dear Lord, I praise You that You are the God who hears. I praise You that You know my heart even before *I* do. I rest in the fact that You are answering my prayer, even before I pray. Help me to be more like You, Lord. So often I don't take the time to listen with love to the people around me. And while they are still speaking, I say *no*. I need Your ears and Your heart, Lord. Speak to me and through me. Amen.

Here Are My Mother and Brothers

Pointing to his disciples, he said, "Here are my mother and my brothers. For whoever does the will of my Father in heaven is my brother and sister and mother."
MATTHEW 12:49–50 NIV

Dear Father, sometimes I feel like I'd do better on a desert island. It's hard to live in community. Our rough edges meet the rough edges of others, and the results are scrapes and sparks and *wounds*. Thank You so much for the pictures You present in the Gospels of Jesus living with His disciples. Lord, nothing teaches me more about what pleases You and what is *possible* than studying how You did it, how You lived and loved and ate and traveled, together. Help me think of the people I rub elbows with as *my* disciples, companions, and teachers. Amen.

DAY 18

A Godly Confidence

Now this is the confidence that we have in Him,
that if we ask anything according
to His will, He hears us.

1 JOHN 5:14 NKJV

Dear Lord, there are so many things I want. Sometimes I feel like my prayers are just a long list of wishes, as though You're some sort of celestial genie. But I'm so thankful You are not. You don't give me what I want, just because I want it. I thank You that You give me only what is in line with Your will for me. So, Lord, show me what that is. Reveal Your will, and show me how and for what You want me to pray.

What Manner of Love

*Behold, what manner of love the Father hath
bestowed upon us, that we should be
called the sons of God.*

1 JOHN 3:1 KJV

A good father protects his children; he loves his children unconditionally; he understands and forgives his children; he provides for his family; he is intimately involved in the lives of those he loves. You are more than a good father, God—You are the *perfect* Father. Remind me, Lord, that *this* is the way You love me. Thank You for loving all of me— unconditionally and without reservation.

Little Altars All Over

*Then let us arise and go up to Bethel,
and I will make there an altar to God Who
answered me in the day of my distress
and was with me wherever I went.*

GENESIS 35:3 AMP

Lord, how easily we forget Your faithfulness. I think *I* would never be like the Israelites, longing for the slave-grown melons and cucumbers of Egypt while following the fire of God through the desert. But my memory is just as short, just as fickle. You knew they needed reminders, so their path was littered with altars and memorials, their calendar marked with feasts and holidays and fasts. *"Don't forget who I Am and what I have done,"* You say. Lord, please show me tangible ways to remember Your faithfulness to me, too. Amen.

DAY 21

Lights

That ye may be blameless and harmless,
the sons of God, without rebuke, in the
midst of a crooked and perverse nation,
among whom ye shine as lights in the world.
PHILIPPIANS 2:15 KJV

Lord, I am grateful that I can claim You as my Father. Because You live in my heart, I am Your representative to the world around me. Thank You for using me for Your purpose, and thank You for filling in the gaps where I am inadequate to do Your work. Make me Your light in the world around me, not so I can gain fame for myself but only to proclaim Your awesomeness.

DAY 22

Good Gifts

"If you then, being evil, know how to give good gifts to your children, how much more will your Father who is in heaven give what is good to those who ask Him!"

Matthew 7:11 nasb

Lord, You are good. You are good! You are a loving, generous God, slow to anger and rich in love. I pray that the riches You offer through Christ Jesus would be visible in my life, so that others would be drawn to You. I have nothing to offer them except You, Jesus. But You have so much, and You long to open the storehouses of heaven to us, blessings pressed down and running over. Amen.

Children of the Resurrection

*Neither can they die any more: for they are. . .
the children of God, being the children
of the resurrection.*
LUKE 20:36 KJV

Because I am Your child, I don't need to be afraid
of death. You Yourself conquered death and the
grave on Easter morning, and You promise me that
Your grace will save me from eternal death as well.
How amazing and wonderful and humbling! I am
so glad, Lord, for the promise of Your resurrection
and the assurance of eternity with You in heaven.
Help me to be bold in sharing this wonderful hope
with people who have no hope.

With This Ring

For no matter how many promises God has made,
they are "Yes" in Christ.
2 CORINTHIANS 1:20 NIV

Dear Lord, You are faithful yesterday, today, and tomorrow. I thank You for giving me a husband who exemplifies that enduring faithfulness. Thank You for how he has kept the promises he made to me on our wedding day: promises to love, cherish, protect, and provide. Thank You for his hands that hold my heart so gently; thank You that he is more like Jesus than anyone I have ever known. I praise You for the great gift that he is to me. Thank You for his example of faithful love, and I pray that I would give him only joy, submission, and devotion in return. Amen.

Alchemy for a Rainy Day

My voice shalt thou hear in the morning, O LORD;
in the morning will I direct my prayer
unto thee, and will look up.

PSALM 5:3 KJV

Dear Lord, it's so dark this morning. I know You've already pushed the sun up over the horizon: it is day, though it doesn't feel like it. I don't want to have to pray this morning, Lord. I just want to be where You are. I don't want to be here, in this gray light, with a longer grayness stretching before me, then darkness again. I want to be with You, walking on streets of gold, with the light of Your glory shining on my face. I long for that endless golden day, Lord. But I am here, and You are not far off. Please come to me, Lord, and shine Your love and light on my heart this morning. Amen.

DAY 26

Peace

Grace unto you, and peace, from God our Father.
2 Thessalonians 1:2 kjv

Thank You, Father, for the gift of Your peace. Help me to remember that Your peace is the only true and lasting rest for my soul—and to always run to You and no other idol in my life. When troubles come my way, please give me an extra dose of Your peace. And when I see others in turmoil, help me to always be ready with a word and an action that will help them seek out Your peace.

Twenty-Four

This is the day which the Lord hath made;
we will rejoice and be glad in it.
PSALM 118:24 KJV

I thank You for this day, Lord, with its twenty-four precious, exhausting hours. Only twenty-four. That never seems like enough, yet I'm always glad to fall into bed when they're over. Some hours spent in sleep, some in work, some in eating, some in talking, some in staring out the kitchen window at the trees and sky. How many of those hours do I give to You, Lord? Not even *one*, maybe two on Sundays? Thank You for continuing to remind me that relationships require *time*, and I vow to give You more of each day—each day that is already a gift from You. Amen.

DAY 28

Falling

Cast your cares on the LORD and he will sustain you; he will never let the righteous be shaken.
PSALM 55:22 NIV

Dear Father, we started falling in Eden, and we haven't hit bottom yet. Today I said some things I regret. And the things I didn't say (the things only *You* heard) were even worse. I hurt people I care about, and worse, I hurt You, Lord. I am so sorry. Please forgive me. Please redeem my angry, selfish words. I am so glad that You tell us in Your Word to forgive seventy times seven times because I know that is how many times You will forgive me. Thanks be to Jesus, when I fall, I am falling into Your arms. Amen.

The Time of Singing

*For lo, the winter is past, the rain is over
and gone. The flowers appear on the earth;
the time of singing has come.*

SONG OF SOLOMON 2:11–12 NKJV

Father, the earth is brown and dead now, as hard as iron and as cold as stone. But I know that life lurks, waits: seeds that will spring to green life with the warming sun and a gentle rain, nests that will hold eggs the color of sky, ponds that will sparkle and sing with dragonflies and frogs. Thank You for spring, for the promise of green and new life. And thank You for heaven, where that fleeting green will never fade and fall away. Amen.

DAY 30

Spirit-Led

For as many as are led by the Spirit of God,
they are the sons of God.

ROMANS 8:14 KJV

Father, let Your Spirit lead me in each thing. Let me always look to You for guidance and direction. Keep me away from the temptation of following the paths of other "gods." Make Your Spirit alive and active in my heart, so that I might hear Your voice every day, in my every decision, and in my every action. Forgive me when I ignore the movement of Your Spirit. Make Him active in my heart, Lord!

The Missing "P"

*"For then you will delight in the Almighty
and lift up your face to God."*
JOB 22:26 NASB

Dear Father, today I just want to praise You! I spend so much time repenting (read: *sinning*), asking (complaining), and yielding (pretending not to be so stubborn), and so little time telling You how much I love You. You are merciful, You are awesome, You are holy! You are beyond compare. You are my Maker and sustainer. You saved me! You are light and love and all that is good. Lord, You made *mountains*. And trees that spear the clouds and birds as bright as rainbows and flowers as small and perfect as a baby's fingernail. Who is like You? Amen and amen and amen.

The Day of Small Things

For who hath despised the day of small things?
For they shall rejoice.

ZECHARIAH 4:10 KJV

Dear Lord, I ask for thankfulness in the small things. I yearn to see each day as a gift—swathed in sunrise—to be unwrapped. Thank You, Lord, for what You gave me today: for a curl of green leaf unfurling on the winter end of a branch, for a cherry blossom like a snag of fuchsia silk, for scratchy frog songs. Thank You for moments that remind me that ordinary days are really shot through with holiness. I thank You now, Lord, for those gifts and the gifts that I will see *You've already given me* as I learn to live in thankfulness. Amen.

DAY 33

Expecting Miracles

Then the fire of the LORD fell and consumed
the burnt sacrifice, and the wood and the stones
and the dust, and it licked up the water
that was in the trench.
1 KINGS 18:38 NKJV

Dear God, I come before You today, knowing You are a God who works miracles. You heal the blind, the lame, the scarred and leprous, and the demon possessed. You crack open prison cells, turn night into day, and roll the ocean up like a scroll. You send down fire from heaven. You bring the dead back to life. I am no Elijah, Lord, but I know You love me. Please answer my prayer today. Work my small miracle. Amen.

Living Words

*O LORD, You are my God. I will exalt You, I will
praise Your name, for You have done wonderful
things; Your counsels of old are faithfulness and truth.*
ISAIAH 25:1 NKJV

Dear God, Your Word is thousands of years old
and tells stories even older. How many books made
millennia ago are still useful today? Curious, maybe,
or *interesting*, but still practical? Lord, I can't think
of even one. We read old poems, histories, and sagas
for school assignments or because we want to learn
about the past or because they tell good stories, but
how many lives have been changed from reading
Beowulf or *The Canterbury Tales*? Your Word is as
true today as when the ink was wet. It is beautiful.
It is inspiring. It is rich. It surprises. It sustains. It
transforms. I praise the living Word.

DAY 35

Peacemakers

Blessed are the peacemakers:
for they shall be called the children of God.
MATTHEW 5:9 KJV

Dear Lord, teach me that if I want the world to see me as Your child, then I need to always work for peace in the world around me. Help me resist the temptation to stir up bitterness or anger among my family, friends, and neighbors. Take away angry, jabbing words that may well up in the heat of the moment. Instead, teach me to be a peacemaker— so that others can't help but acknowledge that You are living and active within me.

The Watcher

The LORD will keep you from all harm—he will watch over your life; the LORD will watch over your coming and going both now and forevermore.
PSALM 121:7–8 NIV

Lord, I'm scared. I'm scared of someone I love getting sick. I'm scared of not having enough money. I'm scared of our country falling apart. I'm scared of being abandoned. I'm scared of hurting the ones I love. I'm scared of stepping on snakes. I'm scared of being laughed at. I'm scared that I'll grow old and die before You return. But mostly I'm scared of never knowing You better than I know You right now. Thank You for that fear, Lord, and how it drives me to my knees again and again. Amen.

DAY 37

Loving Our Enemies

But love ye your enemies, and do good, and lend, hoping for nothing again; and your reward shall be great, and ye shall be the children of the Highest.

LUKE 6:35 KJV

Heavenly Father, You know I have a hard time loving some of the people in my life. Some of them are downright nasty to me. But Your Word says that You want me to repay evil for good. Remind me that You ask me as Your child to not only love my enemies but to also do them positive, active good, without thought of reward. It's not going to be easy, Lord, but with Your help, I can do it.

The Dead Will Live!

But your dead will live, Lord;
their bodies will rise—let those who dwell
in the dust wake up and shout for joy.
ISAIAH 26:19 NIV

Dear Lord, I was feeling so sad this morning. Maybe it was partly the rain and the gray skies, but I was missing certain people so badly. My dad, my grandmothers, my great-aunts, friends. They are all dead, Lord, and that seems so strange and wrong. They are in the ground, out of sight, out of reach. Thank You for comforting me with the assurance that it *is* wrong, that death was not part of Your plan. And that, ultimately, it will be swallowed up in victory. My dad, my grandmothers, they will wake up and shout for joy. Hallelujah!

Praying Like Breath

Rejoice always; pray without ceasing.
1 Thessalonians 5:16–17 NASB

Lord, You gave me life, and I praise You. You filled my lungs with air from my very first breath, and I praise You. I praise You because I am fearfully and wonderfully made. Forgive me for not always loving this body You have given me like the amazing creation and great gift that it is. Today, Lord, I want to pray to You like I breathe: in and out, all day long. Fill my mouth with Your praise. Let my lips be always whispering Your name. Let my heart beat to the rhythm of Your perfect will. Amen.

DAY 40

God's Offspring

For in him we live, and move, and have our being. . . . For we are also his offspring.
ACTS 17:28 KJV

The world tells me to be independent, self-sufficient, and to stand on my own two feet. But the truth is that I am intimately connected to the Lord of the universe, and I rely on You for my life, Father. Most days it's a relief that it's not all on me to handle everything. To put it another way, You and I are kinfolk, Lord! I would not exist if it were not for You.

DAY 41

The Wedding March

He who finds a wife finds a good thing,
and obtains favor from the LORD.

PROVERBS 18:22 NKJV

Dear Father, my kids are all still little and know nothing of romantic desire. They are still in love with me and their father. But I know the day is coming, Lord, when they will transfer their affections to someone else, and I lift those yet-unknown *someones* up to You. Bless their future spouses with faith and wisdom and purity as they wait. I pray that You would help me show my children what marriage can be, and that You would hold their hearts, Lord, until You join them with another. Amen.

Call to Me

"Call to me and I will answer you and tell you great and unsearchable things you do not know."
JEREMIAH 33:3 NIV

O, Lord of the universe, You know everything; You see everything; You are everywhere; You are every*time* and eternal. Lord, sometimes we think that we are so smart, we people that You *made*. Compared to You, we are babies one minute old, looking up at the light and blinking, unable to comprehend anything. But You want us to grow up, Lord. You long to teach us everything You know. I yield my heart and mind to You. Amen.

Who Knows?

*Beloved, now are we the sons of God, and it doth
not yet appear what we shall be.*
1 JOHN 3:2 KJV

Father, I'm grateful for being Your child in this life. I can't even imagine what that will mean in the life to come! Thank You for the hope You have given to me for now and for an unknown future. Although I don't know all the details of what You have in store, I am thankful I can rest secure, knowing You have it all under control.

Make Me Wiser

If any of you lacks wisdom, let him ask of God,
who gives to all liberally and without reproach,
and it will be given to him.

JAMES 1:5 NKJV

Dear Father, today I stumbled up against something that calls for Your wisdom. Someone might be in trouble, Lord. But it's a delicate situation, and I might be wrong. I've been wrong before, You know, and stepped out to offer help without Your blessing and just made things worse. I want to be used by You in people's lives, but first I need Your wisdom. I'm no Solomon, Lord, but just like he did, I'm asking for Your wisdom. Thank You that You promise to give it to me freely and generously. And please protect the woman with the bruised cheek. Amen.

The Confidence of Firsthand Knowledge

I've got my eye on the goal, where God is beckoning us onward—to Jesus. I'm off and running, and I'm not turning back.

PHILIPPIANS 3:14 MSG

Lord, it all comes down to knowing You. Who I am, where I'm headed, and what You require of me all depend on who You are. I don't ask for supernatural revelation, Lord (though I wouldn't turn it down). I just ask for a dogged determination to know You better, verse by verse. I ask—beg, really—for a continual filling of Your Spirit so that my eyes and heart are wide open to You. Then I can say *amen* with confidence. And I will: Amen!

DAY 46

God Is Love

God is love; and he that dwelleth in love
dwelleth in God, and God in him.
1 JOHN 4:16 KJV

God, let me never forget that You are love—patient, kind, not envious, not proud, not rude, not self-seeking, not easily angered, You keep no record of wrong. You do not delight in evil, but You rejoice in the truth. You always protect, trust, hope, and persevere. Your love will always remain. It is the greatest thing there is. May I always make my home within You—within Your love.

The Salvation of Everyone!

For I am not ashamed of the gospel of Christ:
for it is the power of God unto salvation
to every one that believeth.

ROMANS 1:16 KJV

Dear God, sometimes I get weary waiting for You. I am not patient about waiting for the things I long for with all my heart. But I know You are patient, Lord. You are waiting. You are waiting for *us*. Oh, thank You, that You won't return until everyone has had a chance to hear the Gospel. Thank You that Your incredible patience and love is greater than our persistent sin. Who can I tell, Lord? Who is near me who hasn't yet heard or understood the good news? Even so, come, Lord Jesus. Amen.

DAY 48

Wisdom and Might

Blessed be the name of God for ever and ever:
for wisdom and might are his.
DANIEL 2:20 KJV

You, Lord, are all-wise. You make the wisdom of the world look like nothing but foolishness. I will never fully grasp the vastness of Your wisdom, but I am thankful to have that strength in my corner. Scripture says that along with being all-wise, You're all-powerful as well. Speak, and the heavens and the earth are at Your beck and call. No matter how powerful we humans think we are, You are the One who holds it all. Today I "hallow Your name" by relying on Your wisdom and might.

DAY 49

Listen to the Music

The Spirit and the bride say, "Come."
And let the one who hears say, "Come."
And let the one who is thirsty come; let the one
who wishes take the water of life without cost.
REVELATION 22:17 NASB

Dear Father, I'm lifting up a teenager to You tonight who gives You lip service but whose heart doesn't belong to You yet. She knows what to say when Christians are watching, but I know her answers are different when she is in other company. Lord, You are watching her. Remind her of this. Hound her, Lord, until she turns her heart to You. But in this I praise You: she only listens to Christian music. Her soul is yearning for You, whether she knows it or not. Fan that small spark of desire into an eternal *yes.* Amen.

The Cheerleader

I can do all things through
Christ who strengthens me.
PHILIPPIANS 4:13 NKJV

Dear Lord, In this verse I can hear You cheering me on. What can I do? *All things!* Who's going to help me? *Christ!* What's He going to do? *Strengthen me!* I praise You for bringing these particular words to me right now. Your Word is so amazing: written thousands of years ago, yet it speaks to us perfectly in our moment of need. What other book is like that? What other god speaks to his people like You do? I know I am going to need this verse today, Lord. Help me to sing it back to You all day long. Amen.

The God of Hosts

For, lo, he that formeth the mountains,
and createth the wind, and declareth unto man
what is his thought, that maketh the morning
darkness, and treadeth upon the high places of the
earth, The LORD, The God of hosts, is his name.

AMOS 4:13 KJV

God, my Father, You formed the mountains and the wind, the dark of nighttime and the morning's light, and You lead all the hosts of heaven. You formed my intricate features inside my mother's womb. Let me never take for granted Your limitless creativity. Let me never forget who You truly are.

The Construction Site

*Being confident of this, that he who began a good
work in you will carry it on to completion
until the day of Christ Jesus.*

PHILIPPIANS 1:6 NIV

God, I am a work in progress. Sometimes I feel like there should be a barrier of construction tape and a hedge of warning signs up around all my rough edges. I am not who I want to be yet, Lord, and I know I'm not who *You* want me to be. Yet (and this is such a huge relief and amazement) You love me anyway. Thank You for Your mercy today and always and for the sure promise that You *are* carrying out Your work in me. Give me fertile soil and a yielding heart. Amen.

Worry Lines

Don't fret or worry. Instead of worrying, pray.
Let petitions and praises shape your worries into
prayers, letting God know your concerns.
PHILIPPIANS 4:6 MSG

Dear Lord, I praise You for how You are changing me. I praise You for how You are teaching me to place a worry in my open hand and lift it up to You: if it stays or if it flies away, it belongs to You. I trust You with my life. Lord, the only worry lines I want are the creases in the pages of my Bible. I praise You that *You* are the overcomer; *You* are my resting place; *You* are my strength and my fortress. I am so relieved to lay my worries before You and let them become prayers. Amen.

If I Can?!

*Jesus said, "If? There are no 'ifs' among believers.
Anything can happen."*

MARK 9:23 MSG

God, You are so amazing! When You first saved me,
I suddenly felt like the world had shifted under me,
and anything was possible. Even simple, mundane
things such as breathing, eating, and looking up at
the sky were made new. The knowledge that You
did miracles (and might for me, too) made me feel
like I was standing on the edge of a new kind of life
that was so beautiful and grand I might explode
with joy. But it's not just a feeling, Lord. Anything
can happen. I praise You with open wonder. Amen.

Magnifying Glasses

O magnify the LORD with me,
and let us exalt his name together.
PSALM 34:3 KJV

Remind me, Father God, that I am called to be Your magnifying glass. Shine Your light through me to all the world around me. Move me out of the way so that it's all You that others see. My aim is to exalt Your name in everything I do—in thought, word, and deed. Lead me to other people who are like minded so that we can truly live lives that worship You and only You.

Foot Washing

"By this everyone will know that you are my disciples, if you love one another."
JOHN 13:35 NIV

Dear Father, when everything is going well, and people are behaving the way I think they should, I find it easy to love. But when the seas are rougher and the sailors are seasick or muttering mutiny, I am appalled at how quickly I become apathetic or mean spirited. Forgive me, Lord. I want to love like You do. You washed *Judas's* feet! You gently washed the grimy toes of the man who sold You for thirty pieces of silver. What kind of love is that? I could never do that. But Your Spirit, working through my hands, *could*. I praise You for that and so much more.

The Rock

*For the Word that God speaks is alive and full of
power. . .it is sharper than any two-edged sword,
penetrating to the dividing line of the breath of life
(soul) and [the immortal] spirit.*

HEBREWS 4:12 AMP

Dear Father, I have a recurring skeptic in my
life. He won't give up or give in, and nothing I say
seems to make any difference in his opinion of You
or Your Word. He's clinging to nothingness like a
limpet on a rock, and I can't pull him off. Lord, I
am weary of this fight, and I want to give up. But I
know I am here because You put me here with this
stubborn mollusk (whom You love). Please give me
the strength to keep trying, lovingly and gently, to
pry him loose from the big lie he is holding on to.
You are the only Rock. Amen.

DAY 58

Our Redeemer

As for our redeemer, the LORD of hosts is his name,
the Holy One of Israel.
ISAIAH 47:4 KJV

You are my Redeemer, Lord—You have saved me from all that separated me from You. When I am not holy, You are. When I am trapped in anxiety and despair, You free me. When I see no hope of escape from my present circumstance, You rescue me. When I feel unworthy and stained beyond all hope of saving, You cover me with grace. I worship Your name, Your presence, Your beauty, and Your strength.

DAY 59

Baby Blues

He tends his flock like a shepherd: he gathers the lambs in his arms and carries them close to his heart; he gently leads those that have young.

Isaiah 40:11 NIV

Lord, I lift up to You a new mother who is struggling with postpartum depression. With a thirty-six-hour labor, she went from a full-throttle life to a torn body, alien responsibilities, and sleep deprivation. Help her hold on while she heals and adjusts. Surround her with people who will love and support her in practical ways. Be with her husband as he copes with a new baby and a wife who needs him now in ways he never imagined. Bless that little one with health and sleep. Lord, use this time so that they will look back on it and marvel at how You drew them closer to each other and to You. Amen.

The God of Our Salvation

Help us, O God of our salvation, for the glory
of thy name: and deliver us, and purge
away our sins, for thy name's sake.
PSALM 79:9 KJV

When I start to look to other things for my salvation—money, prestige, people, things—remind me, God, that You are the only One who can save me now and keep me safe forever. Remove the temptations from my life that I am so quick to turn to when I'm stressed and insecure. Make me aware of the pitfalls that surround me. Focus my attention on You and Your kingdom.

Who Are Your Philistines?

*"The LORD will cause your enemies who rise
against you to be defeated before your face;
they shall come out against you one way
and flee before you seven ways."*
DEUTERONOMY 28:7 NKJV

I am not a warrior, Lord. I am a weak woman.
You know how many push-ups I can do, how many
miles I can run, how long I can go without rest. But
I have enemies, too. Enemies of anger, self-control,
discontent, pride, selfishness, laziness. Strengthen
me today for my battles against these foes. You are
my high commander, Lord. Strengthen me with
Your Spirit so I will be able to resist the enemy of
my soul and follow only You. Amen.

Don't Touch My Feet

Jesus answered, "Unless I wash you,
you have no part with me."

John 13:8 NIV

Lord, I'm still thinking about foot washing. I can imagine washing someone else's feet, but the idea of having someone—especially You—wash *my* feet makes me squirm. That is appalling grace, like Your offering Yourself up on the cross for us, an act of love so unbelievable that I sometimes don't know what to do with it. How can I say thank You adequately for that? I don't think I ever can. But I will keep trying: thank You, thank You, thank You. Please take away the embarrassment and pride that so often keep me from running to You for the cleansing I desperately need. Amen.

DAY 63

Groaning

*So too the [Holy] Spirit comes to our aid and
bears us up in our weakness; for we do not know
what prayer to offer nor how to offer it worthily
as we ought, but the Spirit Himself goes to meet
our supplication and pleads in our behalf with
unspeakable yearnings and groanings
too deep for utterance.*

ROMANS 8:26 AMP

Dear Lord, my heart and my mind feel empty right
now. I don't know how to pray. I don't know what
to pray. I just feel like a great weight is sitting on
my chest, and I'm afraid the only thing that's going
to come out is a horrible noise filled with tears and
tiredness. Oh, Father. Thank You that You know I
am weak and wordless. Thank You for Your Spirit,
my Comforter. Speak for me. Amen.

How's the Service?

"For the LORD searches all hearts and understands all the intent of the thoughts. If you seek Him, He will be found by you."

1 CHRONICLES 28:9 NKJV

Dear Lord, I do a lot of things for a lot of people every day. I serve, then serve some more. But, Lord, I am asking You right now to show me my heart. Is my service pleasing to You? Am I serving under obligation, as one who is a slave to sin? Or am I serving with the voluntary spirit of my freedom in Christ? I long to serve without counting the cost. But it's so easy to pray this sort of prayer, Lord, and then go and *do nothing*. Please show me who and how to serve, then help me do it in Jesus' name. Amen.

DAY 65

In Temptation

No test or temptation that comes your way is beyond the course of what others have had to face. All you need to remember is that God will never let you down; he'll never let you be pushed past your limit; he'll always be there to help you come through it.

1 CORINTHIANS 10:13 MSG

Dear God, I'm trying to say *no*. Actually I'm trying to say no to this thing You've asked me to stop doing, and I'm trying to say no to You at the same time. I don't want to be double minded, both asking and doubting: I want Your blessing. So, Lord, help me with my temptation. Other people have struggled with exactly what I am struggling with. It is nothing new, only new to me. But You promise in Your Word that I am strong enough. Help me believe and not doubt. Amen.

The Glory of His Name

*Give unto the L*ORD *the glory due unto his name:*
bring an offering, and come into his courts.
PSALM 96:8 KJV

Lord, fill me with the glory of Your name. May I see the splendor and light of Your character everywhere I turn. When I am burdened, show me evidence of Your love in my daily interactions with others and with Your creation. I want to always be ready with God-filled responses to people who ask about my hope.

Get Out of Jail Free

*Whosoever shall call on the name
of the LORD shall be delivered.*

JOEL 2:32 KJV

Father, the world tells me there's no such thing as a free pass. I need to pay my dues, and then someday I may (if I'm lucky) reap the reward. And of course my actions have consequences—the world is quick to remind me of this as well. But, Father, when I am in trouble—when my soul is in captivity—remind me that all I have to do is call Your name. . .and You will set me free.

At Your Nail-Torn Feet

*I have been crucified with Christ and I no longer
live, but Christ lives in me. The life I now live in
the body, I live by faith in the Son of God,
who loved me and gave himself for me.*

GALATIANS 2:20 NIV

Lord, thank You for the story of Ruth. I love
the picture You paint with Boaz, the kinsman-
redeemer, and how he rescued a hungry refugee
girl and gave her the love, prosperity, and hope
she was lacking. And thank You that when You
describe Ruth and Boaz, You are also talking
about me and my Savior. Since I am Your child,
that means Jesus is my kinsman-redeemer, too. I
throw myself at Your feet, Jesus. Cover me with
Your garment of grace. Live in me. Amen.

Majesty and Strength

And he shall stand and feed in the strength of the LORD, in the majesty of the name of the LORD his God.
MICAH 5:4 KJV

Lord, I admit that the stress of life and the burdens of this world often leave me feeling weak and powerless. But Your name is majesty and strength. Your name is higher, more powerful, and far more excellent than anything this world has to offer me. All I need to do is tap into the power of Your name, and You promise to sustain me. I can do all things through You because You give me strength!

The Hollow

Keep me as the apple of your eye;
hide me in the shadow of your wings.
PSALM 17:8 NIV

Jesus, when I think about You making Your home in my heart, I imagine a little creature padding a tree hollow with leaves and dry grasses and turning in a tight, furry circle and falling asleep. The tree is strong—an oak, perhaps, or a towering hemlock—and will stand unbowed through the winter storms. I am that furry creature, Lord: a well-beloved, dear thing. And You are the tree. It is not so much that You live in *me*, but that I live in *You*. Thank You for letting me burrow into Your deep, safe, warm heart, Lord, and remain. Amen.

Jesus, in My Heart

*And I will ask the Father, and He will give you
another Comforter (Counselor, Helper, Intercessor,
Advocate, Strengthener, and Standby), that He
may remain with you forever.*

JOHN 14:16 AMP

Lord, sometimes I think of how the disciples must
have felt after they watched You ascend into heaven:
bereft, terrified, rootless. You had been everything
to them, and suddenly You were gone. *What now?*
they must have wondered. But forty days later, You
were back. Not just for a visit but to *live* in them
forever. Lord, You promise never to leave me or
forsake me, and because of the great gift of Your
Spirit, I know I am not alone. Thank You that You
have made Your home in my heart. Amen.

DAY 72

Singing God's Name

I will praise the name of God with a song,
and will magnify him with thanksgiving.
PSALM 69:30 KJV

God, fill me with Your song today. Orchestrate within my heart a melody that is truly a joyful noise, one that will bring gladness to Your heart. Give me words of praise to You and words of encouragement for others. Fill my song with Your peace and Your beauty. Help me to live out that song every moment, regardless of my circumstances. May I hallow Your name with singing.

In Quietness

*For thus saith the Lord GOD, the Holy One of
Israel; in returning and rest shall ye be saved;
in quietness and in confidence shall be your strength.*
ISAIAH 30:15 KJV

Lord, sometimes it feels like I never sit down. There
are always so many things to do: people to manage,
dishes to wash, bills to pay, groceries to buy, toilets
to fix, e-mails to answer. The noise and busyness of
my life seem unending. But I know You call me to
come away, just as Jesus did, and come to You in
quietness and rest. Not just because You desire it,
but because that quietness and rest in Your presence is the source of my strength. Thank You for
longing to protect my heart in this crazy, merry-go-
round world. Amen.

A God of Justice

*For I the L*ord *love judgment, I hate robbery.*
Isaiah 61:8 kjv

If I hallow Your name, God, then I need to remember just who You really are: a God of justice. Remind me that You have called me to show the same justice in everything I do. Thank You for being the perfect balance of justice and mercy, of fairness and love. Try as I might, I cannot strike that balance in my life without Your help. Teach me to love justice and strive for justice every day.

The Amen Incarnate

*"These are the words of the Amen, the faithful
and true witness, the ruler of God's creation."*
REVELATION 3:14 NIV

Dear Father, so many portraits paint Jesus as a soft, almost wilting, white man. But I bet You weren't: I bet You were dark and as hard as nails. I bet Your feet were cut and Your hands were scarred, even before the cross. Yet You are also the image of the invisible God. You are the Amen, the *so be it*. There is an equation here, the solution of which is just beyond my grasp. Jesus equals the image of God equals Amen equals *so be it*. I am so glad You are not easy to figure out. I am so thankful that You offer mystery and puzzles and food for thought that will satisfy my soul for eternity. Amen.

DAY 76

Face to Grace

And He said to me, "My grace is sufficient for you,
for My strength is made perfect in weakness."
Therefore most gladly I will rather boast in my
infirmities, that the power of Christ may rest upon me.
2 CORINTHIANS 12:9 NKJV

Father, my friend who loves You is dying. Her body is a minefield of cancer; the doctor says she has just weeks to live. Just a few weeks until she sees You face-to-face! But I praise You, Lord, in the midst of my tears because the power of Christ is so visibly resting on her right now, as she stands with her face touching the veil, seeing shadows of the next life. Only You can do this: give a woman, wasting away and saying good-bye to her young family, a joy and strength that evangelizes *others*. Even if You don't heal her, she is giving You all the glory. And I am seeing Your wonders. Amen.

Called by His Name

Thy words were found, and I did eat them;
and thy word was unto me the joy and rejoicing
of mine heart: for I am called by thy name,
O LORD God of hosts.
JEREMIAH 15:16 KJV

Oh God, not only have You adopted me as Your child, but now You say I also have Your name as my own. You pursued me, You purchased me, You accepted me, You love me. Although I don't deserve the honor of being called Yours, I am so happy to accept the gift. Help me strive to be worthy of it.

Strength in Joy

Nehemiah said, "Go and enjoy choice food and sweet drinks, and send some to those who have nothing prepared. This day is holy to our Lord. Do not grieve, for the joy of the LORD is your strength."
NEHEMIAH 8:10 NIV

So often, Lord, I walk around with a glum face, as if being a child of the only living God weren't something to cheer about every moment of every day. I complain about how much work I have to do, how little I am appreciated, how relentlessly hard life seems sometimes. But You tell me in this verse to do these things: eat something yummy (thanks, Lord!), drink, share with others. Since Jesus came to earth, every day is a celebration. And Your festival-joy is the strength I need to keep on. Amen.

So Be It

*The effective, fervent prayer of
a righteous man avails much.*

JAMES 5:16 NKJV

Dearest Lord, I know what I want, but I can't see the future. I know what I think would be best for me and the people around me, but I don't have Your eyes. So I pray, but I hold my prayers lightly. Are they Your will? Am I praying rightly? Show me, Lord. When I pray *Amen*, I think what I really mean is *Your will be done*. And it's a conundrum: I know Your will *will* be done, yet You ask me to pray also. Why, Lord? I long to obey with knowledge, but for now I will simply obey. And wait on You. Amen.

DAY 80

Eating God's Holiness

That we might be partakers of his holiness.
HEBREWS 12:10 KJV

Father, I honor Your name by taking my fill each day of Your holiness. Make Your Spirit alive and active in my heart today. Remind me to always seek You through prayer, meditation on Your Word, and simply being still in Your presence. And when I get "too busy" to take the time to spend with You, please invite me back into Your presence. I can't handle life on my own. . .nor do I want to.

In a Dry Time

On the last and greatest day of the festival,
Jesus stood and said in a loud voice, "Let anyone
who is thirsty come to me and drink. Whoever
believes in me, as the Scripture has said, rivers of
living water will flow from within them."
JOHN 7:37–38 NIV

Dear Father, I want to pray, because You are beautiful and I love You, but the words will not come. I am dry and thirsty. But You are the living water, Jesus. You tell me in Your Word that if I come to You, streams of living water will flow from within me. Thank You for that promise. I am assured that this dry time will not last if I am faithful to come to You for refreshing. I am waiting on You.

Light

God is light, and in him is no darkness at all.
1 JOHN 1:5 KJV

Father God, Your name is light. You have no darkness in Your character. Your brilliance is dazzling—brighter than the brightest star and more beautiful than the most awe-inspiring celestial display. You are a hope-filled promise of never-ending illumination. Please shine on me— and shine *through* me so that others may see the darkness of this world flee before Your light.

The Rock

*The Lord is my rock, and my fortress,
and my deliverer; my God, my strength, in
whom I will trust; my buckler, and the
horn of my salvation, and my high tower.*
PSALM 18:2 KJV

So many names You have, Lord: Rock, Fortress, Deliverer, Buckler, Horn of Salvation, High Tower. All of them tell me that I can trust You absolutely. All of them tell me You are in control, that You will shield me from danger, that I shouldn't be afraid, that I am safe in Your mighty hand. You will never let me down.

Dinner at Jesus' House

"Behold, I stand at the door and knock; if anyone hears My voice and opens the door, I will come in to him and will dine with him, and he with Me."
Revelation 3:20 NASB

Dear Father, I am so blessed that You continue to mold and shape me into the likeness of Your Son. Your Word says that Jesus didn't really have a home of His own. His home was wherever on the road He happened to be when night fell. But today, it hit me that my home, this walled place with bedrooms and tables and bathrooms, really is Jesus' home, too. I ask Your blessing, Lord, as I seek to understand what that kind of a house is like. I ask for Your grace and power to be real in our lives, *here*. Amen.

DAY 85

Truth

Lead me in thy truth, and teach me:
for thou art the God of my salvation;
on thee do I wait all the day.

PSALM 25:5 KJV

Your Son said He was the Way, the Truth, and the Life. Father, may I always walk in Your truth, the truth of Jesus. Teach me patience as I wait for You to move, to act in my life, as I wait for Your return. Waiting is not an easy thing to do, God. Please give me the strength to trust in the hope of my salvation in You. Your truth means everything to me.

DAY 86

Out of Sight

*And when he was demanded of the Pharisees,
when the kingdom of God should come,
he answered them and said, The kingdom
of God cometh not with observation.*
LUKE 17:20 KJV

Father, I can't always see the reality of Your kingdom in the world around me. Give me eyes of faith. Show me the people who are working for Your goals, and give me opportunity to serve alongside them. Allow me to bring Your kingdom to the people and places around me that need You most.

Unwrapping Jesus

*But the gift is not like the trespass. For if the many
died by the trespass of the one man, how much
more did God's grace and the gift that came
by the grace of the one man, Jesus Christ,
overflow to the many!*
ROMANS 5:15 NIV

It's dark, Lord, before the dawn on Your birthday.
I can imagine what this dawn was like two thousand years ago. Mary and Joseph had been up all
night, laboring on the straw, exhausted and filthy
and terrified. Were You born at sunrise? We celebrate Your birth now with tinsel, decorated trees,
and toys. But You came with blood and tears and
terror. My children will be awake soon, Lord, and
I want this day to be different than it usually is.
Help me show them how the gift of Jesus outshines
and outlasts all the glitter. Amen.

Detours on the Way to Amen

*Strengthened with all might, according to his
glorious power, unto all patience and
longsuffering with joyfulness.*
COLOSSIANS 1:11 KJV

Father, I never seem to be able to get to *Amen* in
one go. With people around me all day long (and
no prayer closets with locks), quiet times are
more like dull-roar times. But when I study Your
Word, Lord, I am often so surprised: Jesus going
off alone into the wilderness to pray, then being
followed by the disciples who, like little children,
can't seem to get enough of Him. They interrupt
His prayers with questions and comments, and
He never once says, "Go away, can't you see I'm
praying?" Interrupt me, Lord, and conform my
character into that of Your precious Son. Amen.

Good News

*He went throughout every city and village,
preaching and shewing the glad tidings
of the kingdom of God.*

LUKE 8:1 KJV

Make me Your ambassador, Lord, carrying the good news of Your kingdom to everyone I meet today. Give me new opportunities and new relationships that I might not normally notice, so I can reach more hearts for You. Help me to see these individuals through Your eyes, as loved children of God, created in Your image. Give me the right words to say, and open their ears so they can truly understand the glad tidings of Your kingdom.

Trail Signs

Your ears shall hear a word behind you, saying,
"This is the way, walk in it," whenever you turn to
the right hand or whenever you turn to the left.
ISAIAH 30:21 NKJV

Dear God, I just want to thank You for speaking to me through another believer and keeping me from sin. Lord, You know how I longed to send that e-mail and share something I shouldn't have. I was about to gossip, and I'm sorry. I'm so glad You sent someone to stand behind me and read over my shoulder and gently tell me not to hit SEND. Amen.

Righteousness, Peace, and Joy

For the kingdom of God is not meat and drink;
but righteousness, and peace, and joy
in the Holy Ghost.

ROMANS 14:17 KJV

Remind me, Father, (because I forget so easily) that Your kingdom is not built on the things of this world. The truth is that Your kingdom flies in the face of the things of the world. Righteousness, peace, and joy are heavenly attributes that we humans have a difficult time living out, without Your Spirit to change our hearts. May I not depend on external reality for my satisfaction but instead, dwell always in Your realm of peace and joy.

The Sower

*And he said, So is the kingdom of God, as if a man
should cast seed into the ground.*

MARK 4:26 KJV

God, what does this mean: Your kingdom is like a
man casting seed on the ground? Does this mean
I can find Your kingdom everywhere, scattered
throughout our world by Your generous hand? Give
me new eyes to see Your kingdom all around me,
especially in places I wouldn't expect to see You.
Father, thank You for Your generosity. Thank You
that You do not ever withhold Yourself but are always giving.

Faster, Donkey?

"Be still, and know that I am God."
PSALM 46:10 NIV

Jesus, did You ever hurry? Were You ever in a rush as You walked from Cana to Capernaum? Were You ever late for dinner with Mary and Martha? Did You ever kick Your heels into the donkey's side so it would trot just a bit faster? I don't think so, Lord. Your Word shows You differently: wherever You were was exactly where You wanted to be at that moment, even on the cross. I long to be like that. Please help me slow down and savor this life You have blessed me with: the small moments of glory, quiet words with a friend, even the daily struggles that are conforming me to Your image. I am *here*, and so are You. Amen.

Jesus Lives Here

"Martha, Martha," the Lord answered, "you are worried and upset about many things, but few things are needed—or indeed only one. Mary has chosen what is better, and it will not be taken away from her."

Luke 10:41–42 niv

Dear Jesus, You loved visiting Mary and Martha. Their house must have been a place of comfort, rest, and welcome for You. I wish I could sit at Your feet like Mary did, but then I realize that when I open Your Word, I am. Make my heart welcoming, too, Lord, not a place of sharp corners, cobwebs, and hidden sins. Throw open the windows and let Your light shine in and out. Amen.

A Mustard Seed

*The kingdom of God. . .is like a grain of mustard
seed, which, when it is sown in the earth, is less
than all the seeds that be in the earth.*
MARK 4:30–31 KJV

Lord, in order for Your kingdom to grow and ex-
pand, please plant a seed of faith in my heart.
Make my heart a fertile place for that faith to grow
so that my work in Your kingdom will be fruitful.
Embolden Your Spirit in me so that I might con-
tribute greatly to Your plans—not for my glory but
for Yours alone, Father.

Before the Doorbell Rings

*All the days of the afflicted are evil, but he who is
of a merry heart has a continual feast.*
PROVERBS 15:15 NKJV

Dear Lord, I so wanted to have some quiet moments with You this morning. But the baby woke up early, the plumber called to say he's on his way, and the day is rushing at me down the tracks like a train. But I am going to choose joy today, Lord. I am going to choose to take what You give with open arms. I can pray where I stand, as I walk and talk; I can meditate on Your Word in any and every situation. And maybe I can get up earlier tomorrow! Amen.

Like a Child

*Verily I say unto you, Whosoever shall not
receive the kingdom of God as a little child,
he shall not enter therein.*

MARK 10:15 KJV

Give me a child's heart, Lord. Create in me the
simple and heartfelt belief that You celebrate and
cherish in Your children. Let me experience the
wonder of Your love and gift of grace. Help me to
share with others, with childlike exuberance, the
hope I have in You. Let me set aside grown-up worries and live a joyful life, so that I can enter Your
kingdom.

More Than Just Talk

For the kingdom of God is not in word,
but in power.

1 Corinthians 4:20 KJV

God, sometimes I talk a good game, but my heart and actions don't carry it through. Remind me that Your kingdom is active and powerful. It's not just a bunch of talk. It's real and it's here on earth now. You ask me to help build Your kingdom; show me new ways to serve. Give me a passion for Your kingdom on earth—and for Your heavenly kingdom as well.

After the Amen

"Who among all these does not know that the hand of the LORD has done this, in whose hand is the life of every living thing, and the breath of all mankind?"

JOB 12:9–10 NASB

So, Father, where do I go from here? How do I live once I get up off my knees? I like quick fixes, amazing tricks that promise to solve problems in three easy steps. But I know You are not like that. Sometimes the miraculous intervenes, but more often the Christian life is—as I heard one author put it—a long obedience in the same direction. Maybe what You've shown me most clearly, Lord, is not to wait for everything to be "perfect" before I try to follow You more faithfully. Help me to—standing, sitting, lying down, or running—live as though I'm on my knees. Amen.

Who Holds the Reins?

*All the ways of a man are pure in his own eyes,
but the LORD weighs the spirits. Commit
your works to the LORD, and your
thoughts will be established.*
PROVERBS 16:2–3 NKJV

Dear Father, I spend so much time trying to control others. Futilely. I feel my anxiety mounting, and I know that is not what You want. I can only control my own heart, Lord, and that is only because of Your grace and the gift of Your Spirit. I can't be the "holy spirit" of anyone else's heart. That is Your job. Please help me let go of my agenda and instead lift others up to You. Work on and through *me*, Lord, so they would be drawn closer to You. Amen.

DAY 101

Blessed Poverty

Blessed be ye poor:
for yours is the kingdom of God.
LUKE 6:20 KJV

Lord, make me willing to be poor in this world so that I can be rich in Your kingdom. Give me a spirit of generosity, even giving beyond my comfort level so that I must sacrifice my feelings of security. The things of earth are not the important things, God. I know You will take care of me, and You promise me an even greater reward in heaven.

Falling into Light

I bow my knees before the Father. . .that He would
grant you according to the riches of His glory,
to be strengthened with power through His Spirit.
EPHESIANS 3:14, 16 NASB

Dear Lord, again I thank You for Your precious Word. Thank You for the prayer You gave us in Ephesians 3 and how it has enriched my understanding of You. When I fall to my knees, You will strengthen me. I fall, Lord, because I am weak and because You are great, and then in falling, miraculously, Your strength becomes mine. You dwell in me. Your boundless love bears fruit in me: enough both to keep and to give away. I—weak, broken, sin scarred, blind—am strong, whole, pure, clear eyed, and filled with the fullness of God. Praise God!

Dead and Gone

Jesus said unto him, Let the dead bury their dead:
but go thou and preach the kingdom of God.
LUKE 9:60 KJV

God, help me to let go of the past and look instead to Your future. I know that You hold my past, present, and future in Your hand. I give You all three, and I ask You to be my Savior that covers my past sin, lead me in Your will in my present circumstance, and be with me as I move into Your future. May I not be preoccupied with that which is dead and gone; fill my thoughts and conversation with the reality of Your kingdom in the here and now.

Clean House

So that He might sanctify her, having cleansed her by the washing of water with the Word.
EPHESIANS 5:26 AMP

Dear God, my house is so messy. I just don't seem to have time to get the cobwebs off the ceiling or clean the drips off the fronts of the cabinets or scrub the smudges off the walls around the light switches. Please help me be content with imperfection, because sometimes it seems like I can either clean or read Your Word, but not both. And I know it is far more important to wash the house of my soul with Your living water. Amen.

Healing

And heal the sick that are therein, and say unto them, The kingdom of God is come nigh unto you.
LUKE 10:9 KJV

Your kingdom, Lord, brings healing to those who are sick in spirit, mind, or body. Enable me to carry Your healing to those around me. Keep me accountable; remind me to not just *say* that I will pray for others who are sick but to earnestly and intentionally come to You on their behalf. Help me to see the healing miracles You supply every moment of every day. And remind me to point others to Your goodness in those situations.

The Lord Is in the House

But when the kindness and love of God our Savior
appeared, he saved us, not because of righteous
things we had done, but because of his mercy.
He saved us through the washing of rebirth and
renewal by the Holy Spirit.

TITUS 3:4–5 NIV

Dear Jesus, sometimes I imagine that You are in my house, sitting and watching our activities from the couch like a well-beloved guest. Thank You, Lord, that You care enough to come and stay. God's perfection is blinding and searing and annihilating, and if not for You, Jesus, we would die of it. You are holy (and wholly different) but still a man. I praise You, Jesus, for the sweetness of Your fellowship and the surprising ways You teach us to love. Amen.

Sanctification

For this is the will of God, even your sanctification.
1 THESSALONIANS 4:3 KJV

God, Ruler of my life, You want me to be sanctified—wholly, utterly given to You. I surrender myself to Your will. I give You my heart, my family relationships, my friend relationships, my career, my ministry, my hobbies, my health. Gently prod me along to continue to surrender every area of my life to You—especially the ones that I try so desperately to take back and control on my own. Amen.

DAY 108

Thanks

In every thing give thanks:
for this is the will of God.
1 Thessalonians 5:18 kjv

King of the universe, I give You thanks for all You have given me, every moment of the day. Thanks for the health You've granted that allows me to wake up feeling alert and refreshed. Thank You for the food that nourishes my body to do Your work. Thank You for the clothes You have provided to keep me warm. Thank You for work to do so I may glorify You. Continue to fill my heart with gratitude so that I may do Your will in the world.

A Long Way Off

"When he was still a great way off, his father saw him and had compassion, and ran and fell on his neck and kissed him."

Luke 15:20 NKJV

Dear Lord, I can't even remember where I was three months ago when I began this journey to draw closer to You. I was in a different place; *I* was different. Just like the prodigal son, I am still a long way off. I am far from where You want me and far, even, from where I want to be—and I'm usually pretty easy on myself. But I praise You for drawing me closer. I praise You for how Your Word has soothed the rough, bitter edges of my heart and washed away years of silt and sin. Please help me go forward from here, drinking deeper and believing harder that He who promises is faithful. Amen.

Words, Words, Words

As newborn babes, desire the pure milk of the word, that you may grow thereby, if indeed you have tasted that the Lord is gracious.

1 PETER 2:2–3 NKJV

Dear Father, my life is so full of words: books, TV, movies, neighbors, family, friends, letters, e-mail, advertisements, radio. I am bombarded by them (and bombard others with mine) all day long, and I wonder how many of them really glorify You. And that *is* my desire, Lord: to glorify You. Please help me filter from the filth and froth what is pure and gracious. Help me desire truly to drink only Your pure milk so that it would flow out through me. Amen.

DAY 111

Delight

I delight to do thy will, O my God.
Psalm 40:8 kjv

Thank You, God, that Your will is not one of sadness and gloom. I am grateful that You are not a God that relishes seeing Your children suffer. In fact, You take great pleasure in giving good gifts to me! What a joy to know that You think of me in that way! As I learn to live always within Your kingdom, I am delighted to be able to give back in some small way as I serve You and others.

Time for Healing

He heals the brokenhearted
and binds up their wounds.
PSALM 147:3 NASB

Dear Lord, I find myself obsessing over certain people who upset me, like I'm picking at scabs. I think about how they have wounded me, and those wounds become deeper and sadder. Lord, when I do this, I am pushing Jesus out. I am not letting Him come into these situations and offer His gifts of forgiveness and healing.

Please forgive me for relishing my wounds more than Your healing. Help me pray *for* people instead of muttering against them. I want to know You, Lord, and the power of Your resurrection, even in my small hurts. Amen.

Forever

And the world passeth away, and the lust thereof:
but he that doeth the will of God abideth for ever.
1 JOHN 2:17 KJV

The things of this world never last. I don't know why I get excited about acquiring material things. The anticipation is better than the real thing, which always ends in disappointment. Even my cravings for this world's things come and go. Thank You, Lord God, that Your kingdom is permanent, and I will dwell there forever. Give me a passion for eternity with You—payoff that absolutely will not disappoint!

DAY 114

First Things First

*But seek ye first the kingdom of God,
and his righteousness; and all these
things shall be added unto you.*

MATTHEW 6:33 KJV

You understand, Lord, that I have bills to pay,
deadlines to meet, a house to clean, a family to
care for. These things are important, but they don't
have ultimate importance. Remind me always to
seek Your kingdom ahead of all these things. Give
me a life of balance that is faithfully committed to
Your call. Help me to trust that You will take care
of (and bless) the details of my life.

DAY 115

Joy School

"Come to Me, all who are weary and heavy-laden,
and I will give you rest. Take My yoke upon you
and learn from Me, for I am gentle and humble in
heart, and you will find rest for your souls."

MATTHEW 11:28–29 NASB

Joy is not my native language, Lord. I am more fluent in complaint, agitation, and bitterness. But this tongue of lead is heavy and wearying. I long to speak like the angels at the dawn of creation when they all shouted for joy! This is what I would say: "You are good! You are holy! You are God!" Those are the words that people are dying to hear. Thank You that I am made in Your image, so I can grow and change. I am not an animal, bound by nature; I can learn another tongue. Amen.

Amazing Forgiveness

*In Him we have redemption through His blood,
the forgiveness of sins, according to
the riches of His grace.*
Ephesians 1:7 NKJV

Lord, I come into Your presence, thanking You for forgiveness. In a culture where many experience clinical depression because of guilt, I can know my past is redeemed because of Christ's sacrifice for me. Your forgiveness is so amazing. Although I don't deserve it, You pour it out freely and lovingly. Because You have seen fit to pardon me, I bless Your name today.

DAY 117

Patience

For ye have need of patience, that, after ye have done the will of God, ye might receive the promise.
HEBREWS 10:36 KJV

King of my heart, I want to do Your will. You know that sometimes, though, I grow impatient and filled with doubt. I am distracted by the temptations of the world—money, relationships, power, prestige—that look like answers to my problems. In my heart of hearts, I know they will only lead to ruin. Help me to keep going, relying on You. I know You always keep Your promises.

Heart Transplant

Therefore, if anyone is in Christ, the new creation has come: The old has gone, the new is here!
2 CORINTHIANS 5:17 NIV

Dear Father, You have blessed me with a healthy body, and I praise You for it. I have aches and pains and odd cramps and mysterious rumblings, but I've never had any broken bones, stitches, or spent the night in a hospital for anything except tonsils and childbirth! Thank You, Father. Many are not so blessed. But we all have hidden wounds, Father, wounds that bleed out onto other people. You know what mine are, even better than I do. You are the great Healer, Lord. You heal with a touch, with a word. You heal simply with Your presence. Show me my hurts, Lord, and heal them. Amen.

Enough

God is able to make all grace abound toward you;
that ye, always having all sufficiency in all things,
may abound to every good work.

2 Corinthians 9:8 KJV

You make me sufficient, Lord—You give me enough of everything I need—to carry out Your will. Truth be told, You often supply *much more* than I need. These blessings are wonderful surprises that I don't want to take for granted. Show me ways that I can share Your blessings with others. You are a good giver, Lord. Thank You.

Provisions from God

*You open Your hand and satisfy
the desire of every living thing.*
PSALM 145:16 NKJV

God, there is no creature on earth You do not see
or provide for. I'm bringing praise to You right now
for the daily things You supply for me. It is through
Your goodness that I have food to eat, clothes to
wear, and water to drink. Help me always be
thankful for what I have and to not emulate the
wandering Israelites who, focusing on lack, pre-
ferred to complain. Your power is awesome; thank
You for generously supplying my needs and wants
each and every day.

Rest

*For in six days the LORD made the heavens and
the earth, the sea, and all that is in them,
and rested the seventh day. Therefore the Lord
blessed the Sabbath day and hallowed it.*
EXODUS 20:11 NKJV

Dear Lord, it is Sunday today. Every day is Your
day, but You set aside this one specifically for us,
to rest and worship You. Rest does not come easily to me, Lord. I plan and work and *do*. Resting
seems somehow self-indulgent and lazy. But Your
thoughts toward me are numerous, and higher
than mine. I don't know what I need, but You do.
Plans will be made today; messes will be made.
Help me decide what honors Your commandment
best in each situation: doing or waiting. Help me
make my home and heart places of rest and worship. Show me what that means to You. Amen.

God's Riches

*My God shall supply all your need according
to his riches in glory by Christ Jesus.*
PHILIPPIANS 4:19 KJV

Why should I ever doubt Your ability to give me what I need, heavenly Father, when You have such riches? Your bounty is unfathomable, and You want to share it with me! How humbling! Help me to remember that everything I call "mine" is actually Yours. Forgive me when my heart is hard and unwilling to accept Your riches in glory. Help me to be open to Your Spirit as He moves in my heart.

Pray for Me

The LORD thunders at the head of his army;
his forces are beyond number, and mighty
is the army that obeys his command.

JOEL 2:11 NIV

Dear Lord, how many times have I told someone I would pray for them, then never did? Those were lies, Lord. Forgetting to pray is like leaving a wounded fellow soldier behind on the battlefield. Forgive me. But I need You to help me remember, Lord, for my mind is small and harried and easily overrun. I trust You to be my general and bring them to mind when the fighting is fiercest and the need is greatest. Help me keep my heart and ears open to Your commands. Amen.

No Wants

The LORD is my shepherd; I shall not want.
PSALM 23:1 KJV

Since You are looking out for me—guarding and guiding me—I have everything I need. You are the Good Shepherd who supplies everything to me, Your sheep. Remind me every day that as a sheep, I cannot see the bigger picture—the dangers over the hill or the blessings that are mine to find. Help me more fully trust the Shepherd and His plans for me. Give me a heart of gratitude and a spirit that relinquishes control. Thank You, Lord.

None Like You

"No one is holy like the LORD, for there is none besides You, nor is there any rock like our God."
1 SAMUEL 2:2 NKJV

God, when I consider my own inadequacies, I am amazed at Your perfectness. You are truth and justice, holiness and integrity. There is none like You. You are the one and only true God. Other deities disappoint their followers; other idols fail. But You never do. Because You are perfect holiness, all Your other attributes are only good. There is no selfishness, vengefulness, or deceitfulness in You, Lord. Thus, I can trust You completely and revel in Your light unafraid. Amen.

DAY 126

Seed and Bread

Now he that ministereth seed to the sower
both minister bread for your food,
and multiply your seed sown, and increase
the fruits of your righteousness.
2 Corinthians 9:10 kjv

God, You aren't just a sower or a harvester; You're a true farmer. First You plant the seed; then You water it and nurture it, giving me the food and encouragement I need to grow in You. You work tirelessly to reap a bountiful harvest when my heart is full of fertile soil. I want to return the harvest to You, bearing beautiful fruits of righteousness. Keep working on me, farmer God—I am willing.

Right There with Me

I will praise the LORD, who counsels me;
even at night my heart instructs me.
PSALM 16:7 NIV

Dear God, how many times have I gone to sleep with a problem weighing on my mind and woken up in the morning with a solution that seemed to appear out of nowhere as I slept. I realize now that those miraculous solutions come from You. Thank You, Lord, for counseling me in the night, for instructing me even when I am not aware of it. It comforts me to know that You are so intimately concerned with me, and that even when I don't see Your hand or hear Your voice, You are right there with me. Amen.

Like Birds

Consider the ravens: for they neither sow nor reap;
which neither have storehouse nor barn; and God
feedeth them: how much more are ye
better than the fowls?

LUKE 12:24 KJV

Lord, if You keep track of the lives of birds, then I know I can trust You to watch over my own life. May I rest in the knowledge that You are always looking after me. I know I am worth much more to You than a bird. And even though I know I don't deserve it, I thank You for Your unconditional love.

DAY 129

Priorities

*Therefore I say unto you, Take no thought for your
life, what ye shall eat, or what ye shall drink;
nor yet for your body, what ye shall put on. Is not
the life more than meat, and the body than raiment?*
MATTHEW 6:25 KJV

When I start to worry over little things, help me
to keep my priorities in order, Father God. Give
me grace not to make mountains out of molehills.
Time and time again, You have proven that You
are faithful to take care of me, so what right do I
have to worry? Keep my heart steadfast and my
footing secure in the knowledge that You hold me
in Your hand.

Rooted

*A man is not established by wickedness, but the
root of the righteous cannot be moved.*
PROVERBS 12:3 NKJV

Lord, please forgive me. This has been a hard time,
and I have been entertaining doubts of all sorts.
I am just realizing, as I sit here in the quiet with
You, that I was under attack and I parleyed with
the enemy. I see how the attack went, now: first
pride, then a judging spirit, then self-doubt, then
bitterness, then despair, then an existential doubt
of the foulest sort. *Do You love me? Are You really
there?* I long to grow deep, Lord. I am tired of being
torn out by the roots over and over. Give me the
diligence I am lacking to grow deep in You, down
through streams of living water to the solid Rock.
Amen.

DAY 131

The Inspirational Word

All Scripture is God-breathed and is useful for teaching, rebuking, correcting and training in righteousness.
2 TIMOTHY 3:16 NIV

Lord, Your Word thrills me, convicts me, comforts me, and strengthens me. I am so thankful that You gave us the Bible. Thank You for inspiring the prophets of old as they penned Your truth. Thank You for protecting the scripture through centuries of skepticism and persecution. Thank You for giving me the blessing of this treasure, for allowing me to hold it in my hand. When I am hungry, Your Word feeds me; when I am fearful, it assures me; when I am uncertain, it guides me. Your Book is the light upon my path. Without it, I would be lost. Amen.

DAY 132

Deeper

They have bowed down and fallen;
but we have risen and stand upright.
PSALM 20:8 NKJV

How much is enough, Lord? How deep is deep enough? I read once that the deepest tree roots ever recorded went down well over one hundred feet. I want to be that deep in You. I want the energy of my growth to go downward, not to attractive but weak side branches that just sap my strength. Show me what I need to prune from my life, Lord. Make me willing to clip and snip and shape. Lord, I'm sure Paul's good looks were marred by the beatings, imprisonment, snakebites, and shipwrecks he endured for Your sake, but how firmly he stood! Help me value a firm, rooted faith more than pretty flowers and a pleasing appearance. Amen.

Prayer and Thanksgiving

*Be careful for nothing; but in every thing by prayer
and supplication with thanksgiving let your
requests be made known unto God.*

PHILIPPIANS 4:6 KJV

Even while I'm asking You for something, Lord, I
can already thank You. I know You hear my prayers
and will answer with "Yes," "No," or "Wait." Thank
You for often taking care of my needs even before
I ask. What a comfort it is that You already know
what I need. I can trust You absolutely to answer
me in the best way and according to Your purpose.

Diverse Gifts

There are different kinds of gifts,
but the same Spirit.
1 Corinthians 12:4 niv

Dear God, today the fellowship of other believers ministered to me. There are times when I get frustrated with the church—it has its challenges. But so does a human body. And yet when each bodily organ serves the function for which it was made, there is life, energy, and passion. Help me remember, Lord, that You made my spiritual brothers and sisters with diverse gifts; help me work with them, not against them. Thank You for reminding me again today this family of God is one of Your treasures, a blessing from Your hand—and heart. Amen.

God's Ears

*And if we know that he hear us, whatsoever we
ask, we know that we have the petitions
that we desired of him.*
1 JOHN 5:15 KJV

Thank You, God, that You are always listening to
me. You never ignore my prayers, no matter how
silly or insignificant I think my words might be. It's
a mystery how You can possibly hear the requests
of all of mankind at the same time, but You do!
And each moment of communication is important
to You. Thank You for being a God with always-
listening ears.

Stronger

And we know that all things work together for good to them that love God, to them who are the called according to his purpose.

Romans 8:28 KJV

Lord, You know this is a difficult season in my life. When I was younger, You staked and sheltered me like a precious sapling, but now I am faced with stresses that I never imagined before. Sickness, grief, aging, loss, hardship. But yet I stand. I am amazed at the strength You are giving me daily. Lord, I know myself, and I *know* this is all from You. All these things You are using for Your glory. I know I won't look back from heaven at the events of my life and say anything other than *hallelujah*. I am saying it now. *Hallelujah. Hallelujah.*

Promises

Whatsoever we ask, we receive of him, because we keep his commandments, and do those things that are pleasing in his sight.

1 JOHN 3:22 KJV

Help me to keep Your commandments and always live in a way that pleases You, my Lord. I know Your commandments are not meant to be a burden to me but to keep me safe from harm, from temptations, and to allow me to live in the freedom of Your love. Forgive me for the times I feel like Your laws are constraining to me.

To Every Generation

Your faithfulness endures to all generations.
PSALM 119:90 NKJV

Jehovah God, I come just now to revel in Your faithfulness. From generations past to this very minute, multitudes have testified that You always come through. Yet there have been times in my life when I thought You had overlooked me, that You weren't aware of my needs, that You didn't hear my prayers. But my doubts proved false, and Your record is untarnished. You didn't promise that I would always understand Your ways, but You did promise Your presence and love in every circumstance. And I can testify it's true. I love You, Lord. Amen.

Persistence!

Ask, and it shall be given you; seek, and ye shall find; knock, and it shall be opened unto you.
MATTHEW 7:7 KJV

May I trust You enough, Lord, to ask You for what I need—and then to keep asking, seeking, and knocking until You answer. Help me not to grow weary in coming to You in prayer. I know that You will keep Your promises—that You hear me and are working in the details of my life. When I am praying for others, keep me committed to taking them to You.

Brighter

*The entrance and unfolding of Your words
give light; their unfolding gives understanding
(discernment and comprehension) to the simple.*
PSALM 119:130 AMP

Dear good, gracious heavenly Father, sometimes it is so dark here. Not just the darkness of night or storm or interiors: the darkness of sin and unknowing presses close. I am reaching up for Your light in the only way I can. Thank You, Lord, for Your Word. It comforts and illuminates in a way that nothing else does. It makes You present and real to me. I praise You for giving me something that is so *alive* with Your Spirit to be my anchor and lantern in the darkness. Amen.

DAY 141

Confidence

*Therefore I say unto you, What things soever ye
desire, when ye pray, believe that ye receive
them, and ye shall have them.*

MARK 11:24 KJV

Thank You, Father, that I can come to You in confidence. I am so unworthy to be able to be given access to You through prayer, yet You delight in the communication we have. When I bring requests to You, I want those requests to be things that are not selfish or outside of Your will. Grant that my desires are Your desires, Father. I know that You will always give me whatever I truly need.

Seedlings

And he took the children in his arms, placed his
hands on them and blessed them.
MARK 10:16 NIV

Dear Father, I know my children give You as much joy as they give me, and I just want to thank You for them today. Thank You for their quick minds, their healthy bodies, their loving hearts, their hilarious antics. Most of the time I'm so busy feeding, teaching, disciplining, and organizing them that I don't take even a moment to praise You for what awesome creations they are. Each unique and precious, and each with a soul that will live forever. Give me grace as I continue to point their hearts to You. Amen.

Tomorrow

Take therefore no thought for the morrow: for the morrow shall take thought for the things of itself.
MATTHEW 6:34 KJV

The truth is that I have no control over tomorrow, Lord. Free me from worries about the future, whether tomorrow or next week or next year. May I rely on You today, so that I can focus on the here and now, this moment, and trust You to take care of whatever comes next. I do trust You, Father. Help my actions be evidence to that fact. I yearn for the freedom that comes from being worry-free!

DAY 144

Heart's Desire

Delight thyself also in the LORD: and he shall give thee the desires of thine heart.
PSALM 37:4 KJV

Thank You, God, that You created the deepest, truest desires that live within me. You have made me uniquely different from everyone else, and You've given me a desire to live inside Your will. Thank You for the passions and gifts You have given me. Please show me ways that I can use those gifts to be a blessing to You. I'm glad that as I delight in You, I can trust You always to meet the needs of my yearning heart.

The Past Is Gone

As far as the east is from the west, so far has He removed our transgressions from us.
PSALM 103:12 NKJV

Father, I'm glad You have redeemed my past. I've said and done things of which I'm not proud. I'm grateful that You've blotted out my sins and given me a fresh start. Like one using a marker board, You wiped away the shame and guilt and handed the marker back to me. I don't have to live in the past; I can face the future with confidence and grace. In Christ's name, amen.

Transplanted

Instead, they were longing for a better country—
a heavenly one. Therefore God is not ashamed
to be called their God, for he has
prepared a city for them.

HEBREWS 11:16 NIV

Dear God, You know I am about to move, *again*. Even though this is a move I've been waiting, hoping, and longing for, it will still be stressful. Please be with me in this transition. Amid all the plans and packing, I pray that You would help keep my eyes focused on You. No matter where I put down roots for the next year, or ten or twenty, my true home is in heaven and my true roots in Christ alone. Amen.

Open Up Wide!

I am the LORD thy God, which brought
thee out of the land of Egypt: open thy
mouth wide, and I will fill it.
PSALM 81:10 KJV

Lord, like a baby bird, I will open wide my soul's mouth, knowing that You will always feed me all I need. Open up my heart today, God, and fill it to the brim with just what I need: encouragement, joy, a spirit of servanthood, a passion for the lost, patience, kindness, and a love for others. I'm ready, Father—fill me up!

DAY 148

A Perfect Place

Now I saw a new heaven and a new earth, for the first heaven and the first earth had passed away.
REVELATION 21:1 NKJV

Creator God, I wish there weren't diseases in our world. Those tiny microbes that infiltrate the immune system are responsible for so much pain and grief. Although sickness was not present in the Garden of Eden—that perfect place You intended for us—it is a part of this life now, a consequence of the curse under which our world suffers. But someday You'll create a new earth, and I know bacteria won't stand a chance there. I look forward to that, Father God, for then the world will once again be "very good." Amen.

DAY 149

Satisfied

And the LORD shall guide thee continually,
and satisfy thy soul in drought, and make fat thy
bones: and thou shalt be like a watered garden,
and like a spring of water, whose waters fail not.
ISAIAH 58:11 KJV

Even in the midst of life's droughts—when everything seems dry and dead and dusty—thank You, Father, that You continue to water my heart and satisfy my soul. When I see others are in the midst of drought, give me the right words and actions to share Your living water that will keep them from ever being thirsty again.

Weeds

*For wisdom is better than rubies, and all the things
one may desire cannot be compared with her.*
PROVERBS 8:11 NKJV

Dear Lord, You are the master Gardener. I love to plant flowers, vegetables, bushes, and bulbs, but nothing in my garden can compare with the glory that was Eden. My garden is nothing like that perfection: if I ignore it for two weeks, weeds spring up; in two months it would be a jungle. My life is just like my garden, Lord. Sometimes new things seem insignificant at first: a new TV program, a new book, a new acquaintance, a new train of thought. But they can grow rampantly. Give me wisdom to recognize weeds when they are small and pluck them out. Amen.

Hungry Souls

For he satisfieth the longing soul, and filleth the hungry soul with goodness.
Psalm 107:9 KJV

God, my soul gets so hungry for You sometimes. I know that it's not You who has moved away, but the problem is with me. Thank You that You are immovable, unshakable, and always there. Because of this, I know just where to run to find You, to satisfy my longing soul. Give me a firm footing in Your presence so I am not tempted to wander away again. Thank You for being patient with me.

DAY 152

Internal Clocks

To declare Your lovingkindness in the morning,
and Your faithfulness every night.
PSALM 92:2 NKJV

Heavenly Father, it seems like every person has an internal rhythm seemingly permanently set to a certain time in the day. There are early birds and night owls and middle-of-the-day people. Not many of us are successful in changing our internal clock, Lord. Maybe You wanted to create humans with varying peak hours of energy. It would be a pretty boring world if we all fizzled out at the same time each day. Thank You for the variety You have provided in all of us. Amen.

DAY 153

Rootstock

Know therefore that the Lord your God is God; he is the faithful God, keeping his covenant of love to a thousand generations of those who love him and keep his commandments.

DEUTERONOMY 7:9 NIV

Dear Father, You are a God who is faithful from generation to generation. Thank You for the men and women in my family tree who loved You and passed a godly heritage down to my parents and to me. I praise You that You are the same yesterday, today, and tomorrow: You are the same God Abraham worshipped four thousand years ago, that Paul worshipped two thousand years ago, that my great-grandfather worshipped one hundred years ago. And I praise You that my children and their children's children can follow the same unchanging God. Amen.

DAY 154

Rich in Grace

*In whom we have redemption through his blood,
the forgiveness of sins, according to the
riches of his grace.*
EPHESIANS 1:7 KJV

The world tells me I should be rich in material
wealth, Father, but true riches are found in Your
limitless grace. Thank You for the richness of Your
grace, Lord. Thank You that Your grace is large
enough to cover all my past sin, my current sin,
and my future sin. That's the kind of rich inheritance I truly desire!

Watered

He dawns on them like the morning light when the
sun rises on a cloudless morning, when the tender
grass springs out of the earth through
clear shining after rain.

2 SAMUEL 23:4 AMP

Dear Father, I thank You for things that reach upward, that remind me to lift my arms in praise. Mountains, trees, clouds: they all reach higher than my little arms, but only I can praise You. When I praise You, Lord, I feel so different: washed clean with joy and somehow taller. I feel like a plant after a spring rain. I praise You for the beauty of the earth, the skies, and the heavens, and for Your great love, which surrounds and sustains it all. Amen.

Promises

This is my blood of the new testament, which is shed for many for the remission of sins.
MATTHEW 26:28 KJV

Jesus' blood is the new testament—the new promise You have made to me, Lord. I am not bound by the rules and regulations of the Old Testament law, but instead I have been given amazing freedom! The blood of Jesus is so powerful that I cannot comprehend it, but please help me to always rely on His saving blood that heals all my sins.

DAY 157

Fitness

"Physical training is good, but training for godliness is much better, promising benefits in this life and in the life to come."

1 Timothy 4:8 nlt

It's an exercise-crazy world we live in, Lord. Gym memberships are prized, morning jogs are eulogized, and workout clothing has become a fashion statement. There are some who make this area of self-care too important; they spend an inordinate amount of time on it. Yet others don't keep it high enough on their priority list. Help me, God, to keep the proper perspective of fitness, because, after all, I have a responsibility for the upkeep on this body. It's on loan from You. Amen.

DAY 158

Wilder

By faith Abraham obeyed when he was called to go out to the place which he would receive as an inheritance. And he went out, not knowing where he was going.

HEBREWS 11:8 NKJV

Dear God, today I ask You for strength. I need Your strength to break old habits of sin that are holding me back from the freedom You promise me in Christ. The devil wants me tame: a creature fully at his bidding. Only You, God, give me the capacity to grow and change and stretch. I ask for Your courage today as I abandon old patterns and step past the borders of what is easy and familiar into the wild, beautiful country beyond. Help me to trust that even if it looks like I am the only one following this path, You are guiding me every step of the way. Amen.

Faithful

*If we confess our sins, he is faithful
and just to forgive us our sins,
and to cleanse us from all unrighteousness.*
1 John 1:9 kjv

God, I confess to You that I have sinned. I have gone astray, away from Your love. Again and again I fall short. It shames to me admit it, but You ask for my confession. Forgive me. Wash me. Bring me home. Thank You that even now, I can rely on Your faithful love. Thank You for the promise that You are faithful to forgive me—not just yesterday and today, but tomorrow as well.

Staked

*The eternal God is your refuge and dwelling place,
and underneath are the everlasting arms.*
DEUTERONOMY 33:27 AMP

Lord, the wind is howling like a beast around the house right now. Everything that is not nailed down tight rattles and moans. Our house can stand this much wind, Lord, but how much *more* before it whirls away? Sometimes, Lord, when the wind howls so and reminds me of my frailty, I wonder how long *I* can hold on. How many more tragedies, trials, and temptations? But then You are there, beloved Savior, reminding me of the everlasting arms that are always around me, comforting, sustaining, and protecting. Thank You, Jesus. I stake my life on You. Amen.

Power

*The Son of man hath power
on earth to forgive sins.*
MARK 2:10 KJV

Jesus, no one else has the power to forgive sins like You do. You took the shame of my sins on Your shoulders as You hung on the cross. I cannot understand the immense pain and suffering You endured as You were beaten and ridiculed. You paid for me. You took care of my insurmountable debt. Thank You for Your sacrifice, and thank You for Your power that sets me free from my sins.

DAY 162

Slice of Life

*Make the most of every opportunity
in these evil days.*
EPHESIANS 5:16 NLT

Dear Lord, the transition of minutes to hours is so incremental that it is tedious to observe. It's much easier to focus on a large chunk of time than a myriad of tiny ones. Yet hours are made up of minutes, just like the body is comprised of cells. Each is vital to the whole. Lord, help me remember that each minute of the day is a small section, a slice of my life. Help me make the best use of every minute. Amen.

God's Name

Help us, O God of our salvation, for the glory of thy name: and deliver us, and purge away our sins, for thy name's sake.

PSALM 79:9 KJV

I know that my sins make me dirty, God. More than that, my sins separate me from You. But because You are who You are, You make me clean, Lord. You cover me in the blood of the Lamb, and You deliver me from all my sin so that I may dwell in Your presence. It's nothing that I've done on my own. May I always bring Your name glory!

Nourished

*There are different kinds of gifts, but the same
Spirit distributes them. There are different kinds
of service, but the same Lord. There are different
kinds of working, but in all of them and in
everyone it is the same God at work.*

1 CORINTHIANS 12:4–6 NIV

Dear Father, I thank You for Your church. I have
worshipped You and listened to teaching from Your
Word in so many different buildings, but the same
Spirit has filled them. I know I could walk into any
Bible-believing church in Seoul, Zanzibar, Toledo,
or Des Moines, and feel immediately at home. That
is because You are there, too. I thank You for the
church I am a part of right now. I pray that You
would bless all the people who serve there with extra measures of Your joy, strength, and love this
week. Amen.

A Job for Me

*"But seek first the kingdom of God
and His righteousness, and all these
things shall be added to you."*
MATTHEW 6:33 NKJV

Dear heavenly Father, I need a job. You know the challenges I'm facing in my present situation. You understand the reasons why I need to make this change. There are so many people looking for work; employers have a large pool from which to draw. Still, You've promised to supply my basic needs if I would keep Your kingdom top priority in my life. So, I ask that You would direct my search and help me approach this transition with integrity and consideration for my present employer. I ask this in Your name, amen.

Purged

Iniquities prevail against me: as for our transgressions, thou shalt purge them away.
PSALM 65:3 KJV

I mess up a lot, Father. In fact, sin seems stronger than me sometimes, dear Lord. It takes such a steady foothold in my life that I feel powerless to change. Purge away this tendency from my heart, I pray. I will focus on You and Your Word, Savior God, and I know that You will lead me away from the temptation of sin.

Backsliding

O LORD, though our iniquities testify against us,
do thou it for thy name's sake: for our backslidings
are many; we have sinned against thee. . . . Thou,
O LORD, art in the midst of us, and we are called
by thy name; leave us not.

JEREMIAH 14:7, 9 KJV

No matter how far along I go in my spiritual walk with You, Lord, sooner or later I always start to slide backward. There are some temptations and situations that will always make me struggle, and I admit that sometimes I succumb to those temptations and sin. And yet You are here with me. Don't leave me now.

Gardening

*For the Son of man is come to seek
and to save that which was lost.*
LUKE 19:10 KJV

Dear Lord, other people's lives can be so messy.
Like a teenager's room, it's tempting to close the
door and ignore what is inside. But You are a God
who is not afraid of messes. You are not afraid to
reach into the tangles and the mire. You see into
the future of a lost person's heart: You see a garden
where I only see a dangerous wilderness where *I*
might get hurt—or simply dirty. Lord, I want to be
like You; I want to love the lost like You do. Help
me to look past the mess to the eternal soul inside.
Amen.

Getting Started

The way of the sluggard is blocked with thorns.
PROVERBS 15:19 NIV

Dear Lord, the first step toward any goal is the hardest, and I just don't feel motivated to take it. But there are things I need to do, and so far I haven't found a fairy to do them for me. Procrastination is a terrible hindrance. I know. I'm a closet procrastinator. I don't like to admit to it, but You see it anyway. Thank You for giving me more chances than I deserve. Remind me that I just need to start. Inspiration often springs from soil watered with obedience. Let me learn this lesson well. Amen.

Rebellion

*To the Lord our God belong mercies
and forgivenesses, though we have
rebelled against him.*

DANIEL 9:9 KJV

Sometimes I act like a two-year-old or a teenager—I want to do what I want to do when I want to do it. I disregard what I know is right and good and travel down a dangerous path. Even when I'm in the middle of the situation, I know I'm doing wrong. I rebel against Your love, Lord. Thank You that despite my sheer stupidity, You always forgive me, even though I don't deserve it. Help me never take advantage of Your forgiveness.

Harvest

For this is good and acceptable in the sight of God our Savior, who desires all men to be saved and to come to the knowledge of the truth.

1 TIMOTHY 2:3–4 NKJV

Dear Lord, I thank You that the other night a little girl I love prayed in the dark with her older sister to ask You into her heart. I thank You that other children are asking their friends from school to youth group and that they are getting *saved*. I thank You for the teenagers of a dear friend who love You more than anything in their lives. I thank You for a girl who prays for her grandmother's salvation every day. Lord, the fields are white unto harvest, and You are lifting up faithful laborers even among the little ones. Amen.

Employer Woes

Whatever you do, work at it with all your heart,
as working for the Lord, not for human masters.
COLOSSIANS 3:23 NIV

God, I have the most demanding boss ever. I need to demonstrate the love of Christ, but it can be challenging when my superior is, at times, so hard to please. Give me courage, Lord, to rise above my emotions. Help me pray for my boss as the Bible tells me to and serve as though it is an assignment from You. For You, Lord, are my true superior. Bless my boss today, God, and show Your love to him through me. Amen.

Merciful

I will be merciful to their unrighteousness,
and their sins and their iniquities
will I remember no more.

HEBREWS 8:12 KJV

Thank You that You are a merciful God. You don't even remember all the many times I let You down! You truly forgive and forget. Teach me how to show this kind of mercy to people in my life who have wronged me—that I may shine Your light to others in a real and genuine way, with unconditional love.

Difficult People

*Bear with each other and forgive one another if
any of you has a grievance against someone.*
COLOSSIANS 3:13 NIV

Dear Lord, I ask You to help me be patient and kind today. The Bible speaks about long-suffering. That's what I need as I deal with difficult people and irritating situations. Whether it's squabbling children or rude drivers or harried clerks, I know there will be those today who will irk me. In those moments when I want to scream, help me remember to forbear and forgive. It's just so easy to react, but help me instead to deliberately choose my response. I'm depending on Your power, Father. Amen.

Delighted in Mercy

Who is a God like unto thee, that pardoneth
iniquity, and passeth by the transgression of the
remnant of his heritage? He retaineth not his
anger for ever, because he delighteth in mercy.
MICAH 7:18 KJV

Father, sometimes when I seek Your forgiveness
for a sin that I commit over and over again, I as-
sume that while You are still forgiving me, You
might be doing so begrudgingly. But the truth is
that You delight in mercy! So You delight in forgiving me? What an amazing thought! What would I
do without Your mercy?

DAY 176

Birdsong

"The LORD your God in your midst, the Mighty One, will save; He will rejoice over you with gladness, He will quiet you with His love, He will rejoice over you with singing."

ZEPHANIAH 3:17 NKJV

Lord, I praise You for the little birds in my garden: the chickadees, the robins, the juncos, the purple finches. I praise You for the evening song of the hermit thrush. They are like sequins on a glorious world! You've thought of everything, Lord, and You rejoice in it. Help me remember that as much as I rejoice in songbirds, You rejoice in me even more. Because I am of more value than many sparrows. But thank You for the sparrows, too. Amen.

DAY 177

Blotted Out

I, even I, am he that blotteth out thy transgressions for mine own sake, and will not remember thy sins.
<small>ISAIAH 43:25 KJV</small>

God, I'm so thankful that You don't hold grudges. I give You thanks and praise, dear Lord, for You have not only wiped away all my sins but You also don't even remember them! You wipe my slate clean; You give me a new start; You hit the RESET button. You have made me truly free from the past.

DAY 178

Insurmountable Distance

As far as the east is from the west, so far hath he removed our transgressions from us.
PSALM 103:12 KJV

Whenever I feel that I'm a hopeless case, that I'll never be able to rise above the sin that I fall into, remind me, Father, that from Your perspective, my soul and my sin might as well be in different dimensions, separated by an insurmountable distance. Take away my shame and guilt that I feel about my past sins, and help me rest in the fact that I am completely forgiven.

Googolplex

He telleth the number of the stars; he calleth them all by their names. Great is our Lord, and of great power: his understanding is infinite.

PSALM 147:4–5 KJV

Lord, You are infinite and beyond comprehension. I *know* this with my head, but infinity is such a nonhuman sort of concept! I try to think about You in this way, but my mind keeps trying to reduce You to something smaller, something I can wrap my understanding around. I praise You that You are wholly infinite and infinitely holy. Who is like You? I don't understand, but I rest, a speck in Your loving hand. Amen.

Behind God's Back

Thou hast in love to my soul delivered it from the
pit of corruption: for thou hast cast
all my sins behind thy back.

ISAIAH 38:17 KJV

I have to imagine that if You put something behind Your back, Creator God, it doesn't really even exist anymore. You don't want to look at it, think about it, or even be bothered by it. Always remind me that this is what You have done with my sins! I am free!

DAY 181

Grace in the Not-Knowing

So when. . .this mortal has put on immortality,
then shall be brought to pass the saying that is
written: "Death is swallowed up in victory."

1 Corinthians 15:54 nkjv

Lord, tonight I've cried and cried, and You've listened and loved me and given me words of truth and comfort. But I'm still confused. Someone I love is with You tonight. This morning she was with her husband and children. I wonder why You didn't heal her, because I know You could have and I thought You were going to! Why, Lord? I don't know how to rejoice that she is walking on streets of gold and at the same time weep that her children will grow up without her. But I rest in Your sovereignty, Lord. Please help me live with grace in the not-knowing. Amen

Unlimited Resources

"For every animal of the forest is mine, and the cattle on a thousand hills."
PSALM 50:10 NIV

Father, the Bible says You own "the cattle on a thousand hills." You have unlimited resources. So I'm asking You to supply a special need I have today. Although I try to be a good steward of the money You give me, some unexpected event has caught me without the necessary funds. I know You can remedy this situation, if You deem that good for me. Because You're my Father, I'm asking for Your financial advice. I need Your wisdom in this area of my life. Amen.

The Depths of the Sea

He will have compassion upon us;
he will subdue our iniquities; and thou wilt
cast all their sins into the depths of the sea.
MICAH 7:19 KJV

Thank You for Your loving compassion, heavenly Father, that throws my sin to the bottom of the darkest, deepest ocean—never to be thought of again. Take all the selfish urges of my heart and subdue them, so that I may be free to serve You as I long to.

God Is a Shield

He shields all who take refuge in him. . . .
He trains my hands for battle; my arms can
bend a bow of bronze. You make your
saving help my shield.
PSALM 18:30, 34–35 NIV

Protector God, today I'm remembering someone in the armed forces. Though I know war wasn't in Your original plan for this world, it has become a necessary tool for overcoming evil. The Bible recounts stories of You leading Your people, the Israelites, into battle to defend what was right. So there is honor in defending freedom and justice. I ask You to protect this one from danger; dispatch Your peace, and put a hedge before, behind, and around him. Watch over all those who are putting their lives in harm's way for my sake. In Christ's name, amen.

The Rescue

*"He rescues and he saves; he performs signs and
wonders in the heavens and on the earth."*
DANIEL 6:27 NIV

Dear Father, tonight I watched a movie in which
a sweet but foolish girl was kidnapped and sold
into slavery in a foreign country. No one would
help her, except her father, who crashed through
every barrier and mowed down every bad guy who
stood in his way. Though stabbed, beaten, and broken, he found her and rescued her and brought her
home. I just started weeping, Father, when I realized that *this* is exactly what You have done for
me. I was lost and alone and sold into slavery in
this sin-stricken world. You *came*. You rescued me.
Thank You, again and again. Amen.

New Clothes

Take away the filthy garments from him. And unto him he said, Behold, I have caused thine iniquity to pass from thee, and I will clothe thee with change of raiment.

ZECHARIAH 3:4 KJV

Lord, You offer me a brand-new wardrobe to replace my filthy clothes that are stained with sin. Forgive me when I wrongfully believe that my dirty rags are adequate and I try to hold on to them. Help me put on the new clothes You hold out to me. Dress me in Your love and forgiveness.

Communication

I will set nothing wicked before my eyes.
PSALM 101:3 NKJV

Dear God, the Internet is a marvelous tool! Thank You for giving humankind the ability to invent it. But the Internet also has a great potential for evil. I ask You to protect my family from online predators, from sexual content, from sites that would have a negative influence on our relationship with You. Help me be prudent in my use of the web. Like any other means of communication, it can be used wrongly. But, with Your help, it can be an instrument for good in our home. Amen.

DAY 188

Showered

Then will I sprinkle clean water upon you, and ye shall be clean: from all your filthiness, and from all your idols, will I cleanse you.
EZEKIEL 36:25 KJV

Each time I take a shower, God, remind me that You have showered my soul with Your love. As I lather up with soap that will cleanse the dirt of the day, remind me of the cleansing power of Your grace and mercy. You have washed away everything in me that was false, and now I am truly clean.

Crocuses

*For the L*ORD *thy God bringeth thee into a good*
land, a land of brooks of water, of fountains and
depths that spring out of valleys and hills.
DEUTERONOMY 8:7 KJV

Dear Lord, I just want to praise You today for the
surprising ways You love us. Thank You for the
way rain droplets spangle a branch like diamonds.
Thank You for a stranger's unexpected smile in a
busy store. Thank You for the pictures You paint
every evening at sunset. Thank You for clear, rushing streams and cold drinks of water. Thank You
for the bright heads of crocuses that spring out of
the dregs of winter. Thank You for how You delight
in surprising me with the beauty of Your Word and
Your world. Amen.

Whenever I Pray

And when ye stand praying, forgive, if ye have ought against any: that your Father also which is in heaven may forgive you your trespasses.
MARK 11:25 KJV

Whenever I come to You, Lord, asking You to grant me some request, remind me first to let go of any unforgiveness I'm holding in my heart. I don't want to be a grudge holder, and I know that withholding forgiveness hurts me more than it hurts the other person. Show me ways to show true grace—Your grace—to others who have hurt me.

The Terrible Mercy

"Though he slay me, yet will I hope in him."
JOB 13:15 NIV

Dear Lord, I just finished thanking You for the little moments of beauty You gift me with every day. Then, suddenly, as the sunset faded, the horror of this world seemed to hit me along with the darkness. There are crocuses and raindrops and smiles, but there are also broken bones and broken marriages, breast lumps and biopsies, wars and widows. It's so hard to know what to do with all this beauty so inextricably mixed up with all this viciousness. I am crying out to You. Help me trust Your love even as I try to understand it, Lord. Amen.

A Shining Light

*"Let your light so shine before men,
that they may see your good works
and glorify your Father in heaven."*
MATTHEW 5:16 NKJV

Dear God, I want to be a better witness for You. I have friends and family members who don't know You, and every day I interact with people who aren't believers. Lord, I don't want to be corny or pushy, but I do want to let my light shine before others. I ask You to open up the doors for me today. Let me sense Your prompting. And let the silent witness of my life also speak to others about Your great plan of salvation. In Jesus' name, amen.

Anger Deferred

The discretion of a man defferreth his anger;
and it is his glory to pass over a transgression.
PROVERBS 19:11 KJV

The word *glory* refers to the essence of something, the quality that makes it give forth light. Dear God, remind me that I am most truly myself, my best and shiniest self, when I don't act on my anger against others. Give me the wisdom to know how to react to people and situations in the same way You would react. Let love, respect, and kindness be at the root of everything I do.

Still Learning

Above all, love each other deeply, because love covers over a multitude of sins.
1 Peter 4:8 niv

Lord, I'm really ticked at my husband right now. I just don't get it. How can he be unaware of how his insensitive words hurt me? What I really want to do is quote all those Bible verses to him—the ones that say "love your wives" and "be not bitter" (Colossians 3:19 kjv). But I know You're the only One who can really speak to his heart. Please open his understanding to the way words affect me as a woman. Teach him how to be gentle. And help me remember I'm also a student in relationships. May we both let *You* control the classroom! Amen.

Holes

He also brought me up out of a horrible pit. . . .
He has put a new song in my mouth—praise
to our God; many will see it and fear,
and will trust in the LORD.
PSALM 40:2–3 NKJV

Dear Lord, You know where I was when You found me: at the bottom of a hole so deep even the end of my rope was out of reach. All I wanted to do was pull the dirt down on my own head and die. But You didn't let me. And You didn't just reach down to me; You jumped *in*. Verses, people, hymns, moments of unexpected beauty—they all showed me that You were right there with me, loving me, lifting me. Thank You for changing the ending of my story, Lord, and giving me a tale to tell to the lost. Thank You for the transformative power of Your love. Amen.

Persecution

Do good to them that hate you, and pray for them
which despitefully use you, and persecute you.
MATTHEW 5:44 KJV

Father, bless all those who have hurt me, all those
who have hurt those I love, all those who have hurt
the innocents of our world. I ask that You show me
how to reach out my hands in kind and practical
ways to these individuals who have brought hurt
into our world. Help me to see past their actions to
their own hurt. Use me to show them Your mercy
and love.

Blessings Instead of Curses

Bless them that curse you, and pray for them
which despitefully use you.
LUKE 6:28 KJV

My Lord, I feel misused. I feel cursed. I feel slighted and abused. I'm angry and hurt. I come to You with these feelings, and I give them to You. Take away the hurt and my desire for revenge. Give me Your heart when it comes to others. I pray that You would bless the people who have made me feel this way. Your will be done, Father.

DAY 198

Warming My Hands
by Holy Fire

For our God is a consuming fire.
HEBREWS 12:29 NKJV

Dear Lord, it's so cold this morning. Frost covers the ground, and the air is as still as ice. My fingers are cold, too, but I thank You for a warm cup of tea and a house with a furnace. You always provide for me and protect me, Lord. I never need worry. Thank You that Your love doesn't wax and wane like the warmth of the sun through the seasons. You are a constant and faithful source of light and warmth for my soul. Don't let me grow cold, Lord, but keep my hands pressed up against Your blaze. Amen.

I Blew It

*If we confess our sins, He is faithful and just to
forgive us our sins and to cleanse us
from all unrighteousness.*

1 JOHN 1:9 NKJV

Lord, I blew it today. I was unkind to my
husband and harsh with my kids. I wish I could
take back my attitude and words. Sometimes it's
difficult for me to understand why You still love
me. I am so thankful You would trust me with a
family, even though I've done a pretty terrible
job of nurturing today. Please forgive me. Your
Word promises me cleansing if I confess. Help me
remember this the next time I feel frustrated and
impatient. Help me exercise my will and choose
to respond appropriately to the family You've
given me. In Christ's name, amen.

Inheritance of Blessing

Not rendering evil for evil, or railing for railing:
but contrariwise blessing; knowing that ye are
thereunto called, that ye should inherit a blessing.
1 PETER 3:9 KJV

It's my first reaction to strike back when I'm hurt, to complain against people who complain about me. You know those tendencies within me, Father. Turn them inside out, I pray, and may my first reaction instead be always to pray and bless. When I feel that this is too much to ask of me, remind me that You will give back to me countless blessings in return.

Little Creaks down the Stairs

But it is good for me to draw near to God:
I have put my trust in the Lord GOD,
that I may declare all thy works.
PSALM 73:28 KJV

Dear Father, I can't count how many times I've just sat down at my desk with my Bible and a cup of coffee when I hear the telltale, hesitant creaks on the stairs indicating the approach of a small person who isn't sure of his reception. I confess, Lord, that my heart sinks. But I want more than anything to be like You, and I know that there is never a time when I reach out to You and Your heart doesn't *leap*. I want my children—and the other people around me—to understand the depth of Your love. Help me show them, in part, through the depth of *my* love for them. Amen.

Putting Up with It!

Being reviled, we bless;
being persecuted, we suffer it.
1 CORINTHIANS 4:12 KJV

God, give me patience to put up with all the grief that comes my way! You know the things that push my buttons, that get under my skin. Give me the peace to endure them. I know You will use the situation according to Your will, but it's not so fun to suffer through it! Give me the comfort and encouragement I need to endure.

How Do I Love Thee?

For God so loved the world that He gave His only begotten Son, that whoever believes in Him should not perish but have everlasting life.

JOHN 3:16 NKJV

Dear God, *love* is such a little word, just four letters—a greeting card, fairy-tale, romance novel word. I say *I love hamburgers* with the same verb I would use to say *I love Jesus.* Most of the time I don't think about the power of that word: how it can move mountains, calm storms, heal lepers, redeem a sinner. That word saved me from hell. I remember when I first fell in love, how I longed to hear that word back from my beloved. And that earthly love is just a dim shadow of what You feel for me. I love You, Lord. Let me never stop counting the ways. Amen.

Keep Me

Keep me as the apple of the eye,
hide me under the shadow of thy wings.

PSALM 17:8 KJV

Dear Father, in the scurry of life, I often forget to be thankful for important things. So many times You've shielded my family from physical harm, and I didn't know it until later. And I'm sure I don't even know about all those moments when You've guarded us from spiritual danger. Although we are the apple of Your eye, I realize we're not immune to trauma and disaster; You won't remove the effects of the curse until the right time comes. But for now, I'm grateful that You care about us and that the only way something can touch us is after it's passed Your gentle inspection. Amen.

Feeding My Enemies

*Therefore if thine enemy hunger, feed him;
if he thirst, give him drink.*
ROMANS 12:20 KJV

It's not enough to *forgive* my enemies, Lord; now You ask me to actively do them good—to do whatever I can to meet their needs. I'm hurting so much right now that I can't do this on my own, Father. Show me how You want me to do that, and then give me the strength to do it. May I look for opportunities to help those who have hurt me.

In the Neighborhood

Who is a God like You, who pardons iniquity and passes over the rebellious act of the remnant of His possession? He does not retain His anger forever, because He delights in unchanging love.

MICAH 7:18 NASB

Dear Father, I am surrounded on all sides by people who are dangerously close to spending eternity away from Your presence. They are one misstep (a fall off a ladder, a stumble into traffic) from an eternity they cannot even imagine. I would run into the road to stop a man from being hit by a car; I would scream to wake a woman asleep in a blazing house. But when it's a question of eternity, I say nothing. Open my eyes, Lord, to the moments when the enemy's lying tongue is quiet, and give me Your Words to say. They are just one *prayer* away from an eternity they cannot imagine. Amen.

Waiting for God

Say not thou, I will recompense evil; but wait on the LORD, and he shall save thee.
PROVERBS 20:22 KJV

When a situation arises where wrong has been done, I'm quick to feel that the situation is urgent: I have to do something about it *right now*. Teach me, Lord, to wait for You instead. Give me Your wisdom in these situations, and when the time is right, show me what to say and what to do that will bring glory to You.

DAY 208

Sibling Revelry

Whoever claims to love God yet hates a brother or sister is a liar. For whoever does not love their brother and sister, whom they have seen, cannot love God, whom they have not seen.

1 JOHN 4:20 NIV

Heavenly Father, thank You for my siblings. When the chips are really down, I can depend on them. They know my background, my temperament, and my journey. We share the same blood and the same basic life philosophy. When we were kids, we squabbled a lot; but now, I just love getting a call from one of them. They understand me like no one else. And I pray we'll always be there for one another. Bless my brothers and sisters today. In Jesus' name, amen.

He Is Willing

*Jesus reached out his hand and touched the man.
"I am willing," he said. "Be clean!" Immediately he
was cleansed of his leprosy.*

MATTHEW 8:3 NIV

Dear God, You love us so much that You were willing to leave Your kingly throne and come down into the muck and the sin. For a holy God, sin is *worse* than leprosy. I'm not a leper, *exactly*. My face isn't marred by open sores; I'm not missing pieces of my lips and nose. But sometimes my face *is* mottled by anger, and I'm missing large chunks of the love, joy, peace, patience, kindness, goodness, faithfulness, gentleness, and self-control that are my birthright in Christ. Again and again, You are willing to reach out and touch me and cleanse me with Your amazing love. Thank You, Jesus.

The Other Cheek

Whosoever shall smite thee on thy right cheek,
turn to him the other also.
Matthew 5:39 KJV

Really, God? If someone hurts me, do I really have to ask him to hurt me again somewhere else? That seems like You're asking too much! It goes against everything society teaches me about standing up for myself, about being assertive, about not being a doormat. Teach me what Jesus meant when He said this. Give me a heart that wants to follow His example. . .even when I don't want to.

Following Good

See that none render evil for evil unto any man;
but ever follow that which is good, both among
yourselves, and to all men.

1 Thessalonians 5:15 kjv

Even when I see evil all around me, Lord, help me
to always follow that which is good rather than evil.
Forgive me when I am lured by the fake shininess
and beauty that evil displays. Keep me from falling
for the tricks of the devil, and keep my feet securely
on Your path, the good and right path.

The Promise Keeper

For no matter how many promises God has made,
they are "Yes" in Christ.
2 Corinthians 1:20 niv

Dear Father, how many times have I promised (even just to myself) to call someone and didn't? How many times have I promised to play dolls with my little girl or read a story to my son and didn't? How many times have I promised to get a certain job done and didn't? Forgive me for breaking those promises. You are a God who keeps His promises, who is faithful from generation to generation. Teach me what it means to be truly faithful. Amen.

Role Reversal

"Even to your old age, I am He, and even to gray hairs I will carry you! I have made, and I will bear; even I will carry, and will deliver you."

ISAIAH 46:4 NKJV

Dear Lord, when I was growing up, my parents seemed ageless. But I realize now that my time with them is getting shorter every day. They're getting older, Lord, and, more and more, I find myself looking out for them. This role reversal is really difficult for me. I'm accustomed to them looking out for me, and part of me wishes I could stay in their care for a while longer. Please give me strength to deal with this new phase of our relationship, and help me honor them as long as they live and beyond. Amen.

Love

[Love] beareth all things, believeth all things,
hopeth all things, endureth all things.
1 CORINTHIANS 13:7 KJV

Give me a loving heart, God. Help me to endure hurts, always hoping and believing in the best in others. Remind me that love is an everyday action, not just when I feel like it. Help me show love in words as well. Give me Your eyes to see the true worth of the people around me, and help me always display Your love to them. Thank You for being the perfect example of love.

The Eternal Security System

For He will give His angels [especial] charge over you to accompany and defend and preserve you in all your ways [of obedience and service].
PSALM 91:11 AMP

Dear Lord, Your Word says that we are protected, all unawares, by Your mighty angels. They accompany us and defend us and preserve us when we are walking in Your way. This is not just another security system with a little picture of an angel to stick in our front lawn to deter criminals; they don't just sound an alarm in heaven when our walls have been breached. They keep evil *away*. I know there have been times in my life when You protected me, and I was very aware of it. Thank You, Lord. Thank You also for the invisible guardians that surround me and defend me from the evil I never even see. Amen.

Spiritual Guardrails

Stay alert! Watch out for your great enemy,
the devil. He prowls around like a roaring lion,
looking for someone to devour.

1 Peter 5:8 NLT

Dear God, help me erect proper boundaries in my life. I don't want to fall prey to a sin simply because I wasn't being careful. Just like guardrails on a dangerous mountain highway, boundaries in my life keep me closer to center and further away from the cliffs. I know Satan is plotting my destruction, but Your power is greater. Let me cooperate with Your grace through a careful lifestyle and a discerning spirit. In Christ's name, amen.

Quarrels

Forbearing one another, and forgiving one another, if any man have a quarrel against any: even as Christ forgave you, so also do ye.
COLOSSIANS 3:13 KJV

Quarrels come so easily some days, Lord, especially with the people I live and work with the most closely. Remind me that Christ has forgiven me for far greater offenses, and help me bite my tongue before I start an argument. When I do stumble and take part in a fight, help me be humble and ask for forgiveness from the other person. Grant me freedom in my relationships so I am not distracted by bitterness.

Rule of Love

*"To him who sits on the throne and to the
Lamb be praise and honor and glory
and power, for ever and ever!"*
REVELATION 5:13 NIV

Dear Lord, You are Lord of the universe, yet You left Your throne and came down to earth to be near us. You are the giver and sustainer of life, yet You sacrificed Your Son to save us. You are the King of kings, yet You put aside Your crown to become one of us. There is no precedent for this kind of love. The president of the United States wouldn't sacrifice his child for peace in the Middle East or send his child to live with beggars in India so they could learn about democracy. That would never happen. What You did for us makes no earthly sense. But You did it, and I am forever grateful. Amen.

Tenderhearted

And be ye kind one to another, tenderhearted,
forgiving one another, even as God for Christ's
sake hath forgiven you.

EPHESIANS 4:32 KJV

The world may look at a tender heart as a weakness, but You know better, God. Your heart is tender toward me, and You are quick to extend grace and mercy. Give me a tender heart, I pray. Guard my heart so that it won't become calloused to the hurts and evils of the world. Fill me with Your kindness, gentleness, compassion, and sincerity, so that I can forgive others just as I have been forgiven.

Mother's Day in January

"As one whom his mother comforts,
so I will comfort you."
ISAIAH 66:13 NASB

Dear Lord, I thank You today for my mother. No one else except You has loved me like she has. From before I was born, through sickness and rebellion, and even when I was thousands of miles away, she has loved me. You blessed me so much when You gave me to this particular woman. I praise You for her gentleness, generosity, and quiet strength. I pray that You would bless her today, Lord, with the awareness of how her love and Yours have made a difference in eternity. Amen.

Overcoming

Be not overcome of evil,
but overcome evil with good.
ROMANS 12:21 KJV

When darkness seems to be attacking me from all sides, Lord, give me Your strength so that I can rise above the world's evil. Make Your Spirit strong in me so that I can feel Your presence near. Give me the words to say and the things to do to bring Your goodness to every situation. Use me in whatever way You can for Your will to be done. I know I'm on the winning side!

In Any and Every Situation

From the fruit of their mouth a person's
stomach is filled; with the harvest from
their lips they are satisfied.
PROVERBS 18:20 NIV

Dear Lord, right now my belly is full and my body is
well rested, and I confess that I confuse that physical contentment with spiritual health. And at other
times I have believed the lie that aches, pains, and
sickness mean You have withdrawn Your hand of
blessing from me. Neither is necessarily true, as
You make abundantly clear in Your Word. Paul had
a thorn in his flesh, while the healthy and wealthy
You struck down. Conversely, demons caused sickness, and You blessed Solomon with great wealth.
Help me live in the light of eternity, unswayed
by bank balances, buffets, or blood tests. Amen.

Passion and Purpose

In Him also we have obtained an inheritance,
being predestined according to the purpose of Him
who works all things according to the
counsel of His will.

EPHESIANS 1:11 NKJV

Father, I'm in a rut. I like some familiarity, but this monotony is wearing away at my sense of purpose. I know there are parts of our lives that are not particularly glamorous, fulfilling, or significant (at least, on the surface). Yet living without passion or purpose isn't what You had in mind for us. Show me, Lord, how to find meaning in my everyday life. Open up to my eyes the subtle nuances of joy folded into life's mundane hours. I put my longings into Your hands. Amen.

God's Children

Be ye therefore followers of God, as dear children.
EPHESIANS 5:1 KJV

Brothers and sisters often bicker and squabble. My siblings and I are no exception. But remind me, dear God, that Your children should be following You, not fighting with each other. Grant us an abundance of grace when we are dealing with each other, and help us keep our eyes solely on You as we work through difficulties. If we are following Your will, we will be blessed beyond imagination.

Pascal's Puzzle

Once you were alienated from God. . . . But now
he has reconciled you by Christ's physical body
through death to present you holy in his sight,
without blemish and free from accusation.
COLOSSIANS 1:21–22 NIV

Dear Lord, someone once wrote that there is a God-shaped hole inside every person. I know I felt it, and tried to fill that hole with so many things besides You: work, school, achievement, friends, parties, travel. But nothing was a perfect fit, and the hole remained. But when You found me, even though in pride and fear I tried to say no, the piece that was missing clicked into place. I thank You, Lord, for that hole, for showing me that I was created for something different than a "normal" life. Stop me, Lord, if I lose my first love and start filling that hole with something besides You. Amen.

Merciful

Be ye therefore merciful,
as your Father also is merciful.
LUKE 6:36 KJV

Father, I am so thankful for Your mercy, and I am thankful for Your gift of grace—but You know that it is sometimes difficult for me to show mercy to others. It's especially hard for me to be merciful when I see someone making the same mistake over again or committing the same sin again and again. But right now I pray that You make me like You. Help me show Your mercy to everyone—with no exceptions.

At Dawn in Eden

And they heard the sound of the LORD God
walking in the garden in the cool of the day.
GENESIS 3:8 NKJV

Dear Father, I have always longed to be in the Garden of Eden in those first days when You walked with Adam and Eve in the cool of the day. You enjoyed Your creation; You thought it was beautiful. You enjoyed Your creatures, especially Your people, and You wanted to spend time with them. I am so sorry for what we lost, and I know You are, too. We lost the completeness we had in Eden: we lost that perfect garden and that perfect fellowship with You. But the gift is not like the trespass. Thank You that what You gave us in Jesus Christ is even more beautiful than what we lost. Amen.

Cheerfulness

"Be of good cheer, daughter."
MATTHEW 9:22 NKJV

Jesus, I can't imagine You as a sour, solemn man. I believe You enjoyed life immensely, and I know You brought joy to those around You. Why else would "sinners and tax collectors" want to eat with You (as Your enemies pointed out)? Your mission on this planet was sacred and grave, but I believe Your demeanor in everyday life was buoyant and pleasant. Others loved being in Your presence. Help me pattern my daily attitude after Your example and take heed of Your command to "be of good cheer." Let me reflect You by the way I approach living. Amen.

Semper Paratus

"But rise and stand on your feet; for I have appeared to you for this purpose, to make you a minister and a witness."

ACTS 26:16 NKJV

God, today I have felt like a concrete footing when the forms get removed. Am I dry and sturdy? Will I stand on my own? Will I support a structure above me? I confess that I've been depending on the faith and scripture knowledge of people around me instead of developing my own. When I stand before You, You aren't going to ask whether I was the cousin of a Bible scholar or married to a person of great faith. You will see *me*. I long to hear You say, "Well done." Increase my faith and devotion to You. Amen.

Shielded

*Above all, taking the shield of faith,
wherewith ye shall be able to quench
all the fiery darts of the wicked.*
EPHESIANS 6:16 KJV

Lord, You tell me that my faith is a shield that will protect me from evil. Right now I ask You to reinforce that shield. Give me a greater, stronger faith so that I will be ready when I go through difficult times, when Satan is shooting his fiery darts directly at me. I will not live in fear about this possibility, but I will stand on Your promises.

Essential Jesus

*They replied, "Believe in the Lord Jesus, and you
will be saved—you and your household."*
ACTS 16:31 NIV

Lord, I see in myself the tendency to become a
Pharisee: to add rules to the essential simplicity of
the Gospel. Sometimes I wonder if maybe I need to
dress differently, read only a certain translation of
the Bible, talk with a more specialized "Christian"
vocabulary. But then You remind me of Acts 16:31.
"Believe in the Lord Jesus." "Be saved." That's it.
It's not esoteric knowledge; it's not an unattainable
level of enlightenment; it's not dressing a certain
way; it's not a thousand-mile pilgrimage: it's just
You, Jesus. Help me stay true to this message by
staying close to You. Amen.

God's Gentleness

*Thou hast also given me the shield of thy
salvation: and thy gentleness hath made me great.*
2 SAMUEL 22:36 KJV

Father God, when I think about Your gift of salvation to me, I think about the mighty work that Your grace through the death of Jesus Christ does in my life. But there's another side to it. God, thank You for Your gentleness that makes me strong enough to rise above every trial that comes my way. It's because I am saved that I can be free to stand and not be afraid.

Quiet and Gentle

The unfading beauty of a gentle and
quiet spirit. . .is of great worth in God's sight.
1 PETER 3:4 NIV

God, I read in Your Word that You value spirits that are gentle and quiet. At times, this is oh so hard for me, Lord! I'm not a total pushover, but I do have my own opinions about things. Sometimes it is so hard to keep quiet or speak softly. Yet, Lord, You know that I want to be that way. The universe has enough bossy women. Teach me, Lord, how to be quiet and gentle. Amen.

God's Armor

*But let us, who are of the day, be sober, putting
on the breastplate of faith and love; and for an
helmet, the hope of salvation.*

1 Thessalonians 5:8 kjv

Father, remind me not to venture out into life's
temptations and trials without first putting on
Your armor, especially the breastplate of faith and
love and the helmet of Your salvation. Teach me to
grab hold of these gifts and harness the power that
You offer through them. Give me the opportunity
to use these pieces of armor to bless others, protecting them against the power of evil.

The Already-Done List

*The LORD appeared to him from afar, saying,
"I have loved you with an everlasting love;
therefore I have drawn you with lovingkindness."*
JEREMIAH 31:3 NASB

Dear God, I love plans and schedules. They help me stay focused and productive and turn the 1,440 minutes in each day into goals set and attained. But I know I have missed opportunities to deepen relationships because I was too busy checking off boxes on my to-do list or too rigid to change plans at the last minute. And I know that often I base my idea of how much *I* am worth on how much I have been able to accomplish. Help me remember that I can never *do* enough to earn Your love. I am already loved, completely and eternally. The only thing that really needed doing, You did on the cross. Thank You, Lord.

DAY 236

A Quiet Quest

*"In quietness and confidence
shall be your strength."*
Isaiah 30:15 NKJV

Dear Lord, we all find great blessings when in the company of others, enjoying those times when we are with people. But I need Your help to embrace solitude, too. Let me see the value in spending some time alone, giving my mind time to decompress, refreshing my spirit in the quiet. Not only do I need to spend quiet time with You in personal worship, but I also need to incorporate into my daily routine those pockets of time when the music is off and the computer is down. Help me make times of quiet my quest. Amen.

Lit

Let your loins be girded about,
and your lights burning.
LUKE 12:35 KJV

When everywhere I look I see only darkness,
please, Lord, turn on the lights in my heart. Show
me ways to share that illumination with everyone
around me. When Your light burns, darkness flees.
Use me. Light me, I pray.

Wide Awake

Therefore let us not sleep, as do others;
but let us watch and be sober.
1 Thessalonians 5:6 kjv

You know how tired I am, God. You know how weary I am of facing troubles and challenges. Help me not surrender to my exhaustion. Send godly friends into my life that can encourage me to continue on the path that You have laid for Your children. Keep me wide awake and alert, focused always on You.

Cry in the Night

"Then you call on the name of your god, and I will call on the name of the Lord. The god who answers by fire—he is God."
1 Kings 18:24 niv

Dear Lord, there is never a time I cry out to You and You are not instantly listening. Unlike the false god of the prophets of Baal, You are never busy, traveling, sleeping, or too deep in thought to hear me. The only thing that stops my prayers from reaching You is my own unconfessed sin. Help me examine my heart when I fear that You are silent, and forgive my sins. I long to stand before You, complete and unashamed. Just as I run to my baby when he cries, I know I am never alone. Amen.

Delivered

Because he hath set his love upon me, therefore will I deliver him: I will set him on high, because he hath known my name.

PSALM 91:14 KJV

When troubles threaten to drown me, loving Lord, reach down and save me. Deliver me from the floods. Rescue me from the fire. Remove me from the storm. Protect me from the violence. Pick me up and set me on a high place where I will be safe in Your presence. I know my Deliverer is coming.

Blessed Are the Flexible

This is the day the LORD has made;
we will rejoice and be glad in it.
PSALM 118:24 NKJV

Flexibility is a struggle for me, God. I don't like interruptions in my routine. It's challenging for me to accept a rerouting of my day. Still, sometimes, You have to reorganize for me, because I haven't recognized Your promptings. Or maybe there's someone You need me to meet or a disaster You want me to avoid. Help me accept the detours in my plan today, aware of Your sovereignty over all. Amen.

Preserved

The LORD preserveth all them that love him.
PSALM 145:20 KJV

Preserve me, God; keep me safe—that's what I'm asking of You. Guard my physical body, my head, and my heart. Grant me travel mercies as I move from place to place. Take away my anxiety, my worries, and my woes. I love You—and I need Your help now. I can't do it alone.

The Liar

If we confess our sins, he is faithful and just to
forgive us our sins, and to cleanse us
from all unrighteousness.

1 JOHN 1:9 KJV

Dear God, someone I care about told me a lie today—in church, no less. It was a small lie, about an insignificant thing, but it felt like a brick had been thrown at me. I carried that brick like an ugly goblin baby—a changeling—all through the service, and the music, the sermon, the fellowship of other believers were soured for me because of my burden. Then I realized, Lord, because You so lovingly showed me, that the burden had become mine because I chose to carry it. Thank You for showing me how to lay that ugly thing at the foot of the cross and pick up joy instead. Amen.

True Homeland Perspective

*They agreed that they were foreigners
and nomads here on earth. Obviously people
who say such things are looking forward
to a country they can call their own.*
HEBREWS 11:13–14 NLT

God, I want to live with an eternal perspective. Heaven is more than a feel-good fable for the graveside. It's an actual place, as real as this earth and far more lasting. When I live like this earth is the ultimate goal, I tend toward selfish indulgence. When I remember that heaven is my real destination, I put value on the lasting things, the things of true importance. Remind me to keep an eye toward Your heavenly kingdom. Amen.

The One Needful Thing

I will be fully satisfied as with the richest of foods;
with singing lips my mouth will praise you.
PSALM 63:5 NIV

Dear Father, You are the giver of good gifts, but I confess that I'm often on the lookout for more. I go to the store, Lord, and all the things I see look so nice and necessary. They are just sitting there on the shelves, but in my mind, they are jumping up and down, dancing, and waving to get my attention: *Hey, pick me! No, me! I'll make you happy! I'll make you thinner! Take me with you!* Thank You for the things I have, but help me control my desire for more. No *thing* I have will defile me, but neither will it make me complete. Only You can make me complete, Jesus. Amen.

DAY 246

Alive and Blessed

The Lord will preserve him, and keep him alive;
and he shall be blessed upon the earth: and thou
wilt not deliver him unto the will of his enemies.

PSALM 41:2 KJV

Sickness. . .violence. . .exhaustion. . .stress: our world is full of dangers. Some of the dangers I face are truly life threatening, Lord. But I don't want to live a life of fear. You call me to be bold and fearless. Thank You that You've promised to not only save my life but also to bless me.

The Perfectionist Trap

As for God, His way is perfect.
2 Samuel 22:31 AMP

Dear Lord, I am so glad that You are such a high, mighty, and separate God. I praise You that You are not like the gods of the Vikings or the Greeks, quarrelsome tricksters and schemers. We can only make gods in our own image. We could never imagine You, Lord. I would never bow to Artemis or Baal or Thor, but I realized just now in my perfectionism I am setting up another god to worship—myself. Always doing, striving, perfecting, tweaking my little universe. Please help me be content with imperfection. Only You are perfect, and I am complete, now, in You. Amen.

Never Forsaken

For the Lord loveth judgment, and forsaketh not his saints; they are preserved for ever.
PSALM 37:28 KJV

Father God, I've experienced abandonment in my life. The experience left me feeling empty, alone, helpless. Thank You, Father, that You will never forsake me; You will never abandon me. I am grateful for the security this promise affords me. You will keep me safe forever in Your loving arms that are big enough and strong enough to hold me and all my issues.

Just Do It

But be doers of the word, and not hearers only, deceiving yourselves.
JAMES 1:22 NKJV

Dear Lord, I want to have an obedient heart. Sometimes, when You speak to me, I feel hesitation or want to postpone what You're telling me to do. Yet that means either I don't trust You or I want my own way, neither of which is good. A child ought to obey her parents because she acknowledges their right to direct her and because she trusts the love behind the words. Help me, Lord, to embrace that kind of attitude when You speak to me. In Christ's name, amen.

Saved from All Evil

The LORD shall preserve thee from all evil:
he shall preserve thy soul.

PSALM 121:7 KJV

Evil comes in so many shapes and forms. Sometimes it comes into my life disguised, and by the time I recognize its presence, my soul is already in danger. When this happens, Father, be my rescuer (even when I don't ask for rescuing!). Thank You, Lord, that You are always watching over me—and You will protect me from evil of every kind.

My Hiding Place

Thou art my hiding place; thou shalt preserve
me from trouble; thou shalt compass me
about with songs of deliverance.
PSALM 32:7 KJV

Heavenly Father, when the world seems like a dangerous place, when anxieties rush at me everywhere I turn, be my hiding place. Be by my side and let me run into Your arms. Wrap me up in Your embrace and sing to me Your sweet song of deliverance. May I never think I'm so self-sufficient that I reject Your comfort and protection, Daddy.

Fresh Ink

I lean on, rely on, and trust in Your word.
PSALM 119:42 AMP

Dear Lord, I pray for insight today as I read Your Word. Open it to me, Lord, and reveal Your heart to me. I confess that it has not been my meat and drink as it should. I want to know You better today than I did yesterday, and better tomorrow than I do today. Thank You for the Holy Spirit, who guides me as I read, and I pray for a fresh filling of that Spirit. You make all things new, Lord, and I thank You for the verses I will read today and how they will speak to me, as if You wrote them for me this morning, as if the ink is still wet. Amen.

The Simple Life

*Aspire to lead a quiet life, to mind your own
business, and to work with your own hands.*
1 THESSALONIANS 4:11 NKJV

Dear God, *simplicity* is a buzzword today. It seems everyone wants "simple" in some fashion. Perhaps it's because life has become too complicated for many of us; we yearn for a more laid-back lifestyle. Lord, I need to simplify my goals in my relationships and my work. Doing so will help me to have a more laser-like focus. And in my spiritual life, a little simplifying might be good, too. Instead of daily reading numerous chapters of Your Word, help me to concentrate on one or two verses, thus deepening my understanding of You. Lord, help me keep simple goals and a simple faith as I simply live for You. Amen.

A Tower on a Rock

The God of my rock; in him will I trust:
he is my shield, and the horn of my salvation,
my high tower, and my refuge, my saviour;
thou savest me from violence.

2 SAMUEL 22:3 KJV

You, O Lord, are my place of absolute safety: a high tower built on a rock that will never move. When trials and temptations surround me, teach me to lift my gaze higher. Help me look above all my troubles and see Your tall tower—and then run there as fast as I can!

Mirror, Mirror

*I will praise You, for I am fearfully
and wonderfully made.*
PSALM 139:14 NKJV

Father, when I look at certain people I know, all I see is how much I lack in comparison. They seem naturally kinder, more at ease, more fashionable, more attractive, and certainly thinner. I know, Lord, I often spend more time thinking about how other people see me than about how You see me. You made me, sovereign Lord, in this particular way for Your purposes. Help me trust You, and trust that this lump of clay that You are molding is precious in Your sight and in Your hands. Amen.

The Path to Joy

Keep your lives free from the love of money and be content with what you have.

HEBREWS 13:5 NIV

Lord, I live in a culture that demands more. Wherever I look, I see glossy advertisings of things I "need." It's difficult to be content when you're bombarded with messages to the contrary. But I know that accumulating more stuff isn't the path to joy. And You don't bless me so I can indulge myself, but so I can share with others. Let my life be marked by restraint and a deep contentment that's rooted in You, the center of my fulfillment. In Jesus' name, amen.

My Refuge

The Lord also will be a refuge for the oppressed,
a refuge in times of trouble.
Psalm 9:9 kjv

In times of trouble, Lord, when I feel that the pressure is overwhelming, thank You that You are my Refuge—a place of peace, love, and acceptance. Teach me to seek Your protection at the onset of troubles, rather than trying to handle them on my own. I don't get extra points for trying to stick it out by myself.

DAY 258

Where's Your Missing Piece?

In Him you have been made complete.
COLOSSIANS 2:10 NASB

Dear Lord, the people who still need You don't usually advertise it out loud. They don't usually go around with "Unsaved" or "Missing Jesus" emblazoned on their T-shirts. Sometimes they look just fine, like they aren't missing anything at all. Lord, this is when I feel most uncertain how to tell them about You. I need Your eyes, Lord, to see exactly where and how deep are their "God-shaped holes." Unbelievers are not complete, despite how they may appear. I trust You to lead me, for You love them so much. Amen.

Time Management

Teach us to number our days,
that we may gain a heart of wisdom.
PSALM 90:12 NIV

Dear God, sometimes I think I need more than twenty-four hours in my day! It seems I never have enough time. I think with longing about simpler seasons in my life when I could actually complete my to-do lists. There was such satisfaction in having a few stress-free moments. Now, my schedule is filled, and I'm so harried. Holy Spirit, please guide in this area of my life. How I use my time is part of stewardship, so I'm asking for Your wisdom. Show me how to manage the hours I have so I can honor You in everything I do. In Christ's name, amen.

Singing

*But I will sing of thy power; yea, I will sing aloud
of thy mercy in the morning: for thou hast been my
defence and refuge in the day of my trouble.*

PSALM 59:16 KJV

God, You know all the troubles that surround me—
but today, I'm going to start my day singing. Give
me a song of power and mercy that will stay with
me all day long, especially when the stresses of the
day come. No matter what life throws at me, I want
to live with Your joyful melody in my heart until
Jesus returns to take me home!

Hope

Thou art my hiding place and my shield:
I hope in thy word.

PSALM 119:114 KJV

God, I know that one of the surest ways to find Your hope is to open up scripture and meditate on Your Word. There I learn that You thought of me at the beginning of creation, that You formed me in my mother's womb, that You love me and cherish me, that You provided a way for me to have an intimate relationship with You through the death, burial, and resurrection of Jesus Christ, and that You have amazing plans for me here and into eternity. Your words fill me with amazing hope, Father.

My Prayer Warriors

Always labouring fervently for you in prayers,
that ye may stand perfect and complete
in all the will of God.
COLOSSIANS 4:12 KJV

I thank You, Lord, today for all the people who have prayed for me. I am humbled by how I have been surrounded, from the day I was born, by people who have lifted me up to the throne of grace, faithfully and passionately. I may not ever know who they are, but I ask You to bless them today. Strengthen their faith in the invisible power of their work. I ask that You would bring me to their minds today, Lord, for I covet their intercession. Thank You for these faithful warriors. I need them so desperately. Amen.

Safe in the Midst of the World

*I pray not that thou shouldest take them
out of the world, but that thou shouldest
keep them from the evil.*

JOHN 17:15 KJV

Jesus, You didn't ask that I be physically removed
from the earth, so that I'd be immune to the world's
temptations and tests. Instead, You asked that
God protect me no matter what I face. Thank You,
Jesus, that You prayed for *me*.

The Unveiling

But we all, with unveiled face, beholding as in a mirror the glory of the Lord, are being transformed into the same image from glory to glory.

2 CORINTHIANS 3:18 NASB

Lord, I'm wondering what it really means to be complete in Jesus Christ. What does *complete* really mean, for me? Whole. Absolute. Total. Finished. Accomplished. Concluded. Fulfilled. Done. These are all synonyms, and I am struck by their common sense of finality. There is nothing left to be done. My transformation from stone to flesh was finished at the cross. The work is done; we are just awaiting the final unveiling. Praise Jesus. Amen.

Yes and No

But let your communication be, Yea, yea; Nay, nay: for whatsoever is more than these cometh of evil.
MATTHEW 5:37 KJV

God, teach me Your ways so that no evil will take root in my life. Remind me to make my word count, so that my "yes" means yes, and my "no" means no. Make me a person of integrity that others can trust. When people ask me why I do what I do, let me always point them to You.

DAY 266

The Well of Words

> *"Whoever drinks the water I give them will never thirst. Indeed, the water I give them will become in them a spring of water welling up to eternal life."*
> JOHN 4:14 NIV

Lord, You've given me a love of words, and by Your grace, You've allowed me to use it. Sometimes, though, I worry that I'll run out of things to say. What if the well runs dry? But then I remember how You created everything out of nothing. You spoke, and it came to be. You are the author of life, the Word made flesh. Thank You for breathing that same spark of creativity into us along with the breath of life. I know that if I keep my eyes fixed on You, I'll never run out of words. There is no end to the ways I can praise You! Amen.

Back to Center

*Mark out a straight path for your feet
so that those who are weak and lame
will not fall but become strong.*
HEBREWS 12:13 NLT

Heavenly Father, I need balance in my life. It's one of the hardest things for humans to achieve. We're so prone to lopsidedness, to extremes. Maintaining center is challenging. That's why I need You to straighten me out and help me stay in the narrow way. In those areas of my life where I'm listing to the side, bring me back to center, O Lord. In Jesus' name, amen.

Clothed in Truth

*Stand therefore, having your loins girt
about with truth, and having on the
breastplate of righteousness.*
EPHESIANS 6:14 KJV

Father, this world has exchanged truth for lies.
What You see as black and white, society sees as
gray. Right and wrong has been twisted in such a
way that many people are confused and don't even
know *what* to think. Today I ask that You clothe
me in truth, so that I can live as You want me to.
Give me the boldness to stand up for what is right
and in love guide others to You, the ultimate source
of Truth.

Time Machine

*There is a time for everything, and a season
for every activity under the heavens.*
ECCLESIASTES 3:1 NIV

Dear Lord, I have so much work to do each day and
so little time. I always feel like I'm running behind.
It's a treadmill, Lord, set on a speed that's just a
little too fast for me to keep up; I'm always just on
the verge of flying off the back into a heap on the
floor. But I know this is not what You want. Jesus
was a man who was never in a hurry. He had just
enough time to do the Father's will. He had time to
pray on a mountainside, time to chat beside a well,
time to sit by a lake and cook a fish with friends.
Give me wisdom as I seek to set aside my endless
to-do list for Your holy will. Amen.

Hope to the End

Wherefore gird up the loins of your mind, be sober,
and hope to the end for the grace that is to be
brought unto you at the revelation of Jesus Christ.
1 PETER 1:13 KJV

I have put my hope in Your grace, Lord, which You showed to me through the life of Your Son, Jesus Christ. The account of His death, burial, and resurrection is one that saves me for all of eternity, but meanwhile, I want to emulate His example of grace-filled living now, in my everyday life. Help me always keep His example as my focus.

Hospitality

Use hospitality one to another without grudging.
1 Peter 4:9 kjv

Dear Lord, I need to improve my skills in hospitality. Because You have blessed me, I need to share with others. In fact, hospitality is one of those virtues the apostle Paul commanded of the church. Sharing my home with others is my Christian duty and also a great way to reach out to unbelievers I have befriended. Please let me not dread hosting others but rather find ways to make it doable and enjoyable for all. In Jesus' name, amen.

Firm

*But the Lord is faithful, who shall stablish you,
and keep you from evil.*

2 Thessalonians 3:3 KJV

God, I know You are faithful. Be my Rock and my firm foothold, and please be the foundation of my life. Make me firm and solid, so that I can always resist evil. When my own faith is firmly rooted, then please allow me to help others find their strength in Your faithfulness. Your strength will sustain all Your children!

The Beacon

No one has seen God at any time.
If we love one another, God abides in us,
and His love has been perfected in us.

1 JOHN 4:12 NKJV

My family isn't perfect, Lord. You know how often selfishness, angry words, hurt feelings, and laziness mar our relationships with each other. You know how we are when the door is shut and no one is watching. But we love You, and You are teaching us to love. Increase our love; let it shine out for everyone around to see. Make us a light on a hill, Lord, so that those in darkness would see our Jesus. Amen.

No Slipping

*He will not suffer thy foot to be moved:
he that keepeth thee will not slumber.*
PSALM 121:3 KJV

I'm coming to a situation in my life where the way ahead looks slippery and dangerous, Lord. Please hold my hand, and when necessary pick me up and carry me. I know that You won't leave me or even take a break to get a little rest. Thank You that I can rest in You, even during difficult stretches of the path.

The Real Me

I have chosen the way of truth.
PSALM 119:30 NKJV

Heavenly Father, so many people in my world wear masks. We earth dwellers are afraid to be real with others; we fear losing the respect and esteem of our peers. And, oddly enough, we're often afraid to be real with even You—and You know everything about us anyway. I want to be genuine in my approach and interaction with others, including You. Give me the courage to reject the lure of artificial "perfectness" and instead live out my life and relationships in a real way. Amen.

Cobwebs of the Soul

You will keep him in perfect peace,
whose mind is stayed on You.
ISAIAH 26:3 NKJV

Dear Father, You know how good I feel when my house is in order, when the floors are swept, the bathrooms are clean, the beds are made, and the toys are picked up. It imparts an order and peace to my soul. And You know how I feel when chaos reigns: scattered, bewildered, short tempered. Help me remember that it is no different with my spiritual house. Help me keep the cobwebs and confusion in check with daily prayer, study, and meditation on Your Word. And thank You that I *can*. Amen.

Straight Ways

*Lead me, O Lord, in thy righteousness
because of mine enemies;
make thy way straight before my face.*
PSALM 5:8 KJV

God, You know how hard it is for me sometimes to know which way I should go. Today I ask that You be my map and my guide. Please show me clearly the way You want me to follow. Remind me that You've already "been there and done that." While I may question why we're going a certain way, You know what is best, and You have great plans for me.

Accountability

The LORD will be at your side and will
keep your foot from being snared.
PROVERBS 3:26 NIV

How many times, Lord, have I heard about Christian leaders who fell into great sin. I may have read their books, seen them on TV, and then suddenly their life and ministry crumbled to bits when sin that was hidden came to light. Those leaders probably never imagined where their sin would take them, and I thank You for reminding me that I, too, am capable of any sin. Please protect me, Lord. Surround me with people who will ask tough questions about my life and hold me accountable. I want to be useful to You, Lord, not a broken object of scorn and pity. Amen.

Plain Paths

Teach me thy way, O Lord, and lead me in a plain path, because of mine enemies.
Psalm 27:11 KJV

I need Your help, Lord. I can't see which path I should take. It's dark, I'm confused, and the enemy of my soul has hidden Your way from me. Please, Lord, lead me—and remove the evil that is in the way!

Walking in Truth

Teach me thy way, O LORD; I will walk in thy truth: unite my heart to fear thy name.
PSALM 86:11 KJV

I am guilty of having a divided heart, God. I want to do Your will, but I also want my will to be done. Forgive me for my selfishness. When my heart feels torn with conflicting desires, Father God, please unite me, so that I have a single focus in life: Your way, Your truth, Your will, Your path.

A Dream Deferred Can Bloom

He hath made every thing beautiful in his time.
ECCLESIASTES 3:11 KJV

When I feel small and insignificant, Lord, You so graciously remind me of this verse. When I remember the goals and dreams I had when I was younger that I have not achieved because I chose to follow You instead, You remind me where true worth lies. Thank You for the contentment that only comes from following You. But I thank You, too, for how You are fulfilling some of my old dreams in unexpected ways. I love You, and I trust You completely. If my heart is set on You, then what You give me *will* be the desire of my heart. Amen.

Friends for Every Need

A time to weep, and a time to laugh;
a time to mourn, and a time to dance.
ECCLESIASTES 3:4 NKJV

Dear heavenly Father, I am grateful for my friends. They are such a vital part of my life. When my family can't be there, my friends come through for me. When I need someone to gripe to, they will listen. When I need a kick to get me going again, they don't hesitate. My journey through life would be so lonely and unhappy without these amazing women who walk it with me. Thank You for blessing me through them. Help me return the favor. Amen.

Morning Love

Cause me to hear thy lovingkindness
in the morning; for in thee do I trust:
cause me to know the way wherein I should walk;
for I lift up my soul unto thee.
PSALM 143:8 KJV

It is my desire, Father God, to meet You in prayer every morning. As I start out each day, give me ears, loving Lord, to hear Your voice—and then may I listen for that still, small voice all through my day. Follow me into the evening and whisper loving thoughts to me at night as I rest my head, ready to meet You again in the morning.

Disguises Off!

For now we see through a glass, darkly;
but then face to face: now I know in part;
but then shall I know even as also I am known.
1 CORINTHIANS 13:12 KJV

Lord, You have let me be part of the most amazing thing in the world—Your church. Where believers gather, You are present, and Your glory is made visible. I confess that often I don't even try to look with Your eyes. I see an old building, full of strange people doing odd things. I need to see with Your eyes: that our hundred-year-old church is really a shining fortress, that our creaky voices are a descant to the most glorious choral music in the universe, that the retired accountant in the pew behind me is really a warrior in brilliant armor. And I am something more than I appear. Help me retrain my eyes, Lord, to see as You do. Amen.

God's Eye

*I will instruct thee and teach thee
in the way which thou shalt go:
I will guide thee with mine eye.*

PSALM 32:8 KJV

I have a dog that follows the direction of my gaze and knows what I want her to do. All I need to do is look at her bed for her to go there and lie down; if I look in another direction, toward a treat I've hidden for her, she leaps up and runs to the morsel of food. Lord, help me to be as responsive to Your gaze. Keep me so tuned in to You that You can use Your eyes to show me where You want me to go.

A Caged Bird Singing

*Rejoice to the extent that you partake of Christ's
sufferings, that when His glory is revealed,
you may also be glad with exceeding joy.*
1 Peter 4:13 NKJV

Dear God, I want to thank You for Paul and Silas.
Seized and hauled through the marketplace,
stripped and beaten with rods, thrown into prison—
they prayed and sang hymns from their jail cell.
Your Word says the other prisoners were *listening*
to them: listening and learning what it means to
serve a risen Savior. Nothing like that has ever
happened to me, Lord, and I am very grateful. I
have never felt the terror of a mob; I have never felt
the touch of an angry hand; I have never been in
prison. My trials are ordinary. But I pray that even
still, I would be faithful to praise You in them—
because people are listening. Amen.

Moving and Making Friends

A man who has friends must himself be friendly.
PROVERBS 18:24 NKJV

God, I don't like change or new places. I'd rather just stay in my comfort zone. But that's not happening. Here I am in a strange new environment. I miss my old friends so much. I feel like crying just thinking about them. But that won't do any good, will it? I need some heavenly moxie. It's time to square my shoulders, walk in, smile, introduce myself, and meet some new people. I guess I can think of them as prefriends. Help me not to chicken out! Thank You. Amen.

For My Own Good

*Thus saith the L$_{ORD}$, thy Redeemer, the Holy One
of Israel; I am the L$_{ORD}$ thy God which teacheth
thee to profit, which leadeth thee by the
way that thou shouldest go.*

Isaiah 48:17 KJV

Sometimes I forget, Lord, that Your guidance is always for my good. I admit that sometimes it feels a little bit like taking my medicine. But You want what's truly best for me. Your paths always lead me to joy and blessing and health. Teach me to trust You more fully today and every day.

DAY 289

Open Ears

And thine ears shall hear a word behind thee,
saying, This is the way, walk ye in it, when ye turn
to the right hand, and when ye turn to the left.
ISAIAH 30:21 KJV

Give me sharp ears, heavenly Father, so that I can
hear Your voice. Tune my ears to be receptive to
only You, and give me discernment so I can disregard the false voices that may try to imitate You.

DAY 290

The Proof Is in the Pudding

*"Then you will know the truth,
and the truth will set you free."*
JOHN 8:32 NIV

Dear Father, we are a gullible people. From the very beginning, we were tricked and led astray. Satan whispered in Eve's ear, she listened, and everyone ever since has been falling for his lies. *Just this once. It's doesn't really matter. I deserve this. No one will find out.* We believe his lies about everything from eating too much chocolate, to "borrowing" a pencil from work, to committing adultery or murder. I am no different. I need You every moment, Lord, to help me sort through the chatter in my head so I can be certain what to listen to and what to stand against. Only the truth. Only what glorifies You. Amen.

Reconciliation

Be kind to each other, tenderhearted,
forgiving one another, just as God
through Christ has forgiven you.
EPHESIANS 4:32 NLT

Dear Lord, I feel as if I'm on the set of *I Love Lucy* today, starring in an episode in which Ethel and Lucy have had a quarrel. I just can't believe that my friend and I had this disagreement. It feels so odd to have a chill between us instead of the warm camaraderie we've always shared. I confess I'm still hurt over what she said. Maybe she feels the same about the words that came out of my mouth. So please help us both to take the steps toward reconciliation. What do You want me to do right now to start repairing this friendship? Amen.

No More Crooked Ways

I will bring the blind by a way that they knew not; I will lead them in paths that they have not known: I will make darkness light before them, and crooked things straight. These things will I do unto them, and not forsake them.

<small>ISAIAH 42:16 KJV</small>

Sometimes my life's path seems to take one unexpected turn after another. I feel as though I'm stumbling through a dark maze. One day, though, Lord, when I look back at my life from heaven's perspective, will I see that You made my life's crooked paths run absolutely straight, right to You?

Little Mary, Quite Extraordinary

*"For He who is mighty has done great things
for me, and holy is His name."*

LUKE 1:49 NKJV

God, thank You so much for Mary, this nobody of a
girl from nowhere who became the mother of God.
I thank You for her amazing example of humility
and exuberant praise. She never drew attention to
herself; instead, everything she said glorified You.
She lived a poor, quiet life but found favor in Your
eyes and became a witness to the Incarnation, the
defining event of history. Only You, Lord, delight
in turning our expectations on their head this way!
Help me be more like Mary, Lord, and say continually, "Let it be to me according to Your word."
Amen.

The Path of Life

Thou wilt shew me the path of life: in thy presence is fulness of joy; at thy right hand there are pleasures for evermore.

PSALM 16:11 KJV

Why do I think I'm a trailblazer, Lord? Sometimes my way seems better to me, so I take a little side trip off Your path, only to find disappointment, destruction, and heartbreak. I know that only Your path, God, leads me to life. . .to joy. . .to pleasures that will last forever. I will put blinders on my eyes, Father—looking straight ahead to You.

Faithful Friendship

Faithful are the wounds of a friend.
PROVERBS 27:6 NKJV

Father, I need to confront my friend. She seems to be making some bad decisions. I'm so afraid for her. Please keep me from joining in the discussions of others who are talking about her. Yet my just being silent isn't what she needs. I know some things about her life that have brought her to today; I know her secret pain and longings. Let me not betray her but rather come alongside to share the burden she's carrying and perhaps lovingly suggest another solution than the one she's trying. Heal her heart, Lord, and give me guidance in the process. In Christ's name, amen.

Lifting Weights of Sin

"Forgive, and you will be forgiven."
LUKE 6:37 NIV

Dear Lord, I am struggling to forgive. I don't want to: I want to hold on to my resentment and continue to look at it and pet it and admire it. Help me, Lord. Each time I do this, Lord—allow You to come into a situation and help me forgive—it feels like the hardest thing I have ever done. I lay my burden at the cross, and suddenly I feel lighter. But then after a few minutes, or hours or days, I walk over and pick it up again. How could You do this for billions of people, when I can't even forgive *one* person and have it stick? I am looking to You, Jesus. Help me carry my cross daily in forgiveness and follow You. Amen.

Standing Up Straight

Teach me to do thy will; for thou art my God: thy spirit is good; lead me into the land of uprightness.
PSALM 143:10 KJV

My burdens have been feeling extra heavy lately, Father. I am still walking along Your path, but maybe You've noticed my shoulders slumped, my head hung low. Gently remind me that I don't need to carry these burdens—that You are strong enough to carry all the weight of the world. I give You my worries and woes, Father. Help me to stand upright and follow the path of Your perfect will.

DAY 298

Mentoring

*May [the aged women] teach the young women to
be sober, to love their husbands,
to love their children.*

TITUS 2:4 KJV

Dear God, the Bible tells older women to mentor
younger women. That's an element missing from
my life. Although my mom did a great job of pass-
ing along the life lessons she'd learned, and we
have a good relationship, I still need the insight
and affirmation of an older woman. Lord, I need a
trusted confidante, one who will help me succeed. I
ask You to send someone like that my way in fulfillment of Your Word. And let me fill that role myself
someday when I have the required résumé. Amen.

Everlasting Ways

See if there be any wicked way in me,
and lead me in the way everlasting.
PSALM 139:24 KJV

You know, Lord God, how easily I hide selfishness inside my heart. But try as I might, I cannot hide it from You. Shine Your light on all my blind spots. Show me where I need to grow and change to be more like You. Bring true godly friends into my life that can help me in these areas. Lead me in the path that will lead me to eternity.

Instructions in Righteousness

"But I tell you, love your enemies and pray for those who persecute you, that you may be children of your Father in heaven."
MATTHEW 5:44–45 NIV

On the same note, Lord, I want to thank You for this verse in Matthew. When You tell us to pray for our enemies (or even those we're just annoyed with), it works. I quite literally can't hold on to my negative feelings about a person when I'm lifting them up to You. Your Word is powerful, and, when I obey it, I feel Your power at work in me. When I feel crushed by the weight of unforgiveness, like I don't have a hope or a prayer, this verse offers me both: it gives me a specific prayer to pray and tells what will happen if I do. I want to be Your child. Thank You for showing me how. Amen.

The Same Old Me

You have searched me, Lord, and you know me.
Psalm 139:1 niv

Lord, today I come to You a bit discouraged. The traits I see in myself are ones I don't like. It seems I could do much more for You without some of the inherent flaws of my personality. So help me overcome my defects, or please use me in spite of them. Help me love myself, as imperfect as I am, and strive to be the best me I can be. I know You can find a way around my impediments and use me for Your glory, just like You used Moses in spite of his speech problem. Amen.

Future Glory

*For I reckon that the sufferings of this present
time are not worthy to be compared with the glory
which shall be revealed in us.*

ROMANS 8:18 KJV

When it comes down to it, God, it's not all about
me. I am guilty of being so selfish, self-centered,
"me focused" that I lose perspective of the big picture. Father God, when pain surrounds me, give
me a glimpse of the glory that lies ahead. Help
me regain a proper sense of perspective. Show me
where You want me in Your will!

Eternal

For our light affliction, which is but for a moment,
worketh for us a far more exceeding
and eternal weight of glory.
2 CORINTHIANS 4:17 KJV

When I think about eternity, God, I realize that the time I spend on earth is pretty insignificant. But I still get so focused on my daily problems, Lord, that they seem insurmountable. Burdens and worries eat away at my joy, Lord. Instead, I choose to yield myself to whatever comes into my life and rely on Your power to get me through. Use my problems and troubles to transform me for eternity, I pray.

Forgive

You are from God, little children, and have overcome them; because greater is He who is in you than he who is in the world.

1 JOHN 4:4 NASB

Forgive me, Lord, for harping on the same subject over and over. I am so slow to learn the lessons You are teaching. But You are patient and loving. . .and *long-suffering*. Thank You for not giving up on me as I learn to forgive others. I remember the first time You helped me win this battle. I remember being in the car, alone, and yelling, "I can't forgive him! I won't!" But You just kept insisting, quietly and firmly, *"Forgive."* And then I did. I forgave and felt Your joy flood my heart. And I was *stronger*. Help me remember this victory, Lord, and keep strengthening my muscles for the harder battles to come. Amen.

Not Good Enough

I praise you because I am fearfully
and wonderfully made.
PSALM 139:14 NIV

Father, shopping for clothing at the mall makes me so insecure. The store windows are filled with posters of glamorous women in size 0 clothing. I feel I will never "measure up" to these airbrushed supermodels. Like every other twenty-first-century woman I know, I struggle with body image. Although these feelings of inferiority seem petty, and a bit self-centered, they are so real sometimes that I get depressed. I know that isn't what You want for me. Help me with these feelings and show me the way to triumph over them. In Christ's name, amen.

Blessed Hope

Looking for that blessed hope,
and the glorious appearing of the great
God and our Saviour Jesus Christ.

TITUS 2:13 KJV

Some days, Father, I hold on to a single thread of hope. But the hope You offer through Jesus Christ is real and active, and even when it's wearing thin, it sustains me. The hope I have in You, God, is for the future—but it blesses me today. Fortify my hope so that I can share it with other weary travelers in this world. Help me direct them to the true source of hope.

Timely Wisdom

*For the Lord gives wisdom; from His mouth come
knowledge and understanding.*
PROVERBS 2:6 NKJV

Lord, I wasted my time this afternoon watching
a movie. I needed to do other things, but I got
caught up in the plot. Now I'm running behind in
my schedule. Thank You, Lord, for giving writers
and moviemakers the gifts necessary to craft mov-
ing stories, sometimes life-changing dramas. But
help me to use my time more wisely so I can enjoy this pleasure sans guilt. And, Lord, help me to
guard my mind carefully when I'm selecting what
to watch. Amen.

When Christ Appears

When Christ, who is our life, shall appear, then shall ye also appear with him in glory.
COLOSSIANS 3:4 KJV

Jesus, I look forward to Your return to earth. I'm so thankful that I am not on my own—that You are with me all the way. Thank You for the gift of Your Holy Spirit that lives in me and empowers me with the strength necessary to live for God. You are my life now, and You will take me with You into glory, where I will be made perfect.

A Bowl of Rice, Please

But godliness with contentment is great gain.
1 TIMOTHY 6:6 KJV

Dear Father, there has never been a nation so blessed with *things* and opportunities and peace as this one. I don't know why You chose to let me live here, rather than, say, Angola or Eritrea or Afghanistan, but *thank* You. Yet, we are a nation with so many wants, and I am no different. Where someone in another country might want enough rice to fill his belly, a quiet night's sleep, or a doctor to treat his infected leg, we want another outfit to stuff in a jam-packed closet, the newest techno-gadget, and a house with a pool. It will never be enough, Lord. Only You can fill the hole we try to fill with stuff. Thank You that I want for nothing except contentment. Amen.

The Power of Words

Death and life are in the power of the tongue:
and they that love it shall eat the fruit thereof.
PROVERBS 18:21 KJV

Father, my mouth sometimes gets me into trouble. Please keep me aware of the things I say that aren't right. Let me back up and apologize if I've hurt anyone. Better yet, let me consider my words before I cast them out on the wind. Once spoken, they can never be recalled. Your written Word is living, brilliant, and powerful; Jesus is the embodiment of it—the Living Word. My spoken earthly words are weighty as well; they can minister life or death to those who hear. I ask You to remind me of this throughout the day. Amen.

God's Thoughts

For I know the thoughts that I think toward you,
saith the LORD, thoughts of peace, and not of evil,
to give you an expected end.
JEREMIAH 29:11 KJV

God, You know how easily my thoughts turn to worries and fears. Teach me to think Your thoughts instead: thoughts of peace and goodness that will lead me into the future You have planned for me. Show me the steps I should take to reach the abundant life You have in store for me, both here on earth and in eternity.

DAY 312

The Pebble

"You did not choose me, but I chose you and
appointed you so that you might go and bear
fruit—fruit that will last."
JOHN 15:16 NIV

Sometimes I feel like I have no influence, Lord.
That nothing I think or do resonates much beyond
the walls of this house. But You comfort and em-
power me with Your Word again. Thank You for
reminding me that no matter what small circles we
move in, we are all leaders to someone: a child, a
wife, a younger brother, a boy flipping burgers in
a fast-food joint, a shy new believer in church. I
am a tiny pebble thrown into the sea, Lord, but my
ripples will travel. Amen.

DAY 313

Before the World Began

In hope of eternal life, which God, that cannot lie,
promised before the world began.
TITUS 1:2 KJV

Think of it, Father! You are a God that cannot lie—
there is no falsehood or deceit in You. Your promises are better than gold and they reach forward
into eternity—and they reach backward, before the
heavens and earth were made. There is no place in
time's long arc where You are not, so why should
I worry about past, present, or future? Hold me in
Your hand today.

God's Riches

*Oh, the depth of the riches both of the wisdom
and knowledge of God! How unsearchable are His
judgments and unfathomable His ways!*
ROMANS 11:33 NASB

When I start to worry about my life, Father, when
I start to feel as though You may not know what
You're doing—remind me that Your riches are far
greater than my needs. Give me a spirit of peace
when I don't understand the whys, secure in my
faith that You are doing a good work that will bring
glory to Your name.

The Missing Link

Then God said, "Let there be light"; and there was light. God saw that the light was good; and God separated the light from the darkness.
GENESIS 1:3–4 NASB

Dear Lord, sometimes I have to laugh at how hard people work to explain life apart from a Creator. They are desperate to throw their lot in with amoebas in a primordial soup pot rather than with a loving, creative God who might require something of them. But I thank You that You did create the universe out of nothing and us out of the dust of the earth. You spoke light into existence. Not in a billion years could we design a universe so complex, detailed, and interlocking. Thank You for the amazing love that keeps it all spinning. Amen.

DAY 316

All Grace

The God of all grace, who hath called us unto his eternal glory by Christ Jesus, after that ye have suffered a while, make you perfect, stablish, strengthen, settle you.
1 Peter 5:10 kjv

I'm glad, God, that Your grace is so wide and great that it can work even through this life's pain and suffering. Give me the right amount of comfort to endure those times of pain and suffering, and remind me that in the end, I can count on You to make me perfect and strong, settled in Your love forever.

Abundance

*[God] is able to do exceeding abundantly above all
that we ask or think, according to the
power that worketh in us.*
EPHESIANS 3:20 KJV

Father, I often put limits on what is possible in my
life—to my own detriment! Help me recall the miracles You've done in my life—the "God incidents"
that have Your fingerprints all over them. Remind
me to share these fantastic stories with others so
they too might learn to see You at work in their
lives. Give me Your eyes to see the endless power
You have at work in me. May I expect Your abundance to fill my future.

Obsidian

*The Lord liveth; and blessed be my rock; and
exalted be the God of the rock of my salvation.*
2 Samuel 22:47 KJV

Lord, my house is full of the flu, but I praise You
with a kind of wide-eyed joy. I feel *patience* (where
did *that* come from?) thickening like a skin over
the lava of my usual anger, and I know that it can
only come from You. I walk gingerly, Lord, because
I don't yet trust myself. Will I fall through? Is it
thick enough to hold? But thank You for what You
are slowly forming beneath my feet: solid rock.
Amen.

No Spirit of Fear

*For God hath not given us the spirit of fear; but of
power, and of love, and of a sound mind.*

2 Timothy 1:7 kjv

Father, I deal with a phobia. It isn't anything life
threatening, but it's embarrassing. I haven't told
anyone, and I'm hoping I never have to. But I ask
You now to help me; I don't want my phobia to keep
me from living the life You've planned for me. Help
me to bring this fear to You; show me that You are
in control, that You are the security system in my
life. I ask this in Jesus' name, amen.

Shining More and More

The path of the just is as the shining light, that shineth more and more unto the perfect day.
PROVERBS 4:18 KJV

Father, when I am in vibrant fellowship with You, the path before me seems clearer and Your will seems more evident. Thank You for the light that shines brighter with each step I take. When the light seems dim or I'm not sure which way to go, bring me back into Your presence and lead me to Your holy Word. Thank You for never giving up on me, Father.

Pack Nothing but Faith

Now faith is the assurance of things hoped for, the conviction of things not seen.
HEBREWS 11:1 NASB

Dear Lord, Your world is so beautiful and *large*. Sometimes I sigh for all the places I will never see before I die. Mount Everest flying its white cloud-flag of spindrift. Greek islands floating in a wine-dark sea. A blue morpho flickering through the black-green-gold of the jungle. I miss them, somehow, though I've never seen them. But I know that nothing good will be lost, and I am confident that in heaven, I will ache for nothing left behind. I praise You for what *is* and for what will be. Amen.

Fixing My Thoughts

*Fix your thoughts on what is true, and honorable,
and right, and pure, and lovely, and admirable.*
PHILIPPIANS 4:8 NLT

God, today I'm having a pity party. My thoughts
are so focused on earthly things that I am having
trouble looking up. I could mope around here all
day, but I guess it's time for the music to stop and
the party to end. Lord, You can't work through
me when I'm feeling sorry for myself. Forgive me
for my pettiness, and let me respond to life with
maturity. Help me focus on good, praiseworthy
things. In Christ's name, amen.

Like Jesus

Beloved, now are we the sons of God, and it doth not yet appear what we shall be: but we know that, when he shall appear, we shall be like him; for we shall see him as he is.

1 John 3:2 KJV

God, You promise that You're not done with me yet. In fact, I won't be finished until You come again to the earth and take me home with You. It doesn't really matter what my future holds, God, so long as one day I will be like Jesus.

Face-to-Face

*For now we see through a glass, darkly; but then
face to face: now I know in part; but then shall I
know even as also I am known.*
1 CORINTHIANS 13:12 KJV

You know that I can't see You clearly, Father. You
know I don't really understand You, even when I
am seeking You every day. I'm grateful, though,
that I expect to see You face-to-face—and that on
that day, I will finally truly know You even more
intimately and personally than now. What an
awe-inspiring promise!

Flu Season

The LORD will strengthen him on his bed of
illness; You will sustain him on his sickbed.
PSALM 41:3 NKJV

Now the flu's got me, too, Lord, and I feel like I'm
hanging on by the skin of my teeth, whatever that
means. But You use everything to draw us closer to
You, and even in this I can see You. Though I feel
terrible right now, this virus will run its course; in
a day or two I'll feel well again. But I won't *really*
be well because I am also infected with another
terrible disease, Lord, which will only be healed
in glory: sin. I praise You, Comforter, Healer,
Sustainer, for what You are doing right now in my
body and what You *will* do when I see You face-to-
face. Amen.

Fadeless Beauty

*The unfading beauty of a gentle and quiet spirit,
which is so precious to God.*
1 PETER 3:4 NLT

Dear God, I'm getting older. That's not news to You, I know. You've seen my journey from day one. But now my body is revolting, and my hormones are rebelling. I don't like looking in the mirror because it shocks me to see lines on my face. Inside I don't feel old, but my body doesn't agree. Still, Lord, help me remember that my identity in You is changeless, and my beauty in You is fadeless. The magazines may say differently, but I know that in Your sight, I have a loveliness that time can't touch. Amen.

Glory to Glory

*But we all, with open face beholding as in
a glass the glory of the Lord, are changed into
the same image from glory to glory,
even as by the Spirit of the Lord.*

2 CORINTHIANS 3:18 KJV

You have given me glory in this world, God. You
have given me splendor and light. You have created
my very essence so that it shines. And as I keep
my eyes on You, You are creating within me even
greater glory. May Your Spirit work in my heart,
God, so that I am transformed into Your image.

Unblemished

And He who sits on the throne said,
"Behold, I am making all things new."
REVELATION 21:5 NASB

Lord, I praise You today for babies, for the gift of new life and the new life I have in You. I marvel at the perfect, round cheeks of my baby, his skin so smooth and firm and kissable. His silky hair lighter than air, his wide, bright eyes. When he smiles, his face is all joy. Do You see me this way, Lord? Do I bring You this much joy? Sometimes I have a hard time believing that I—with my sags and bags and scars—am fearfully and wonderfully made. But I trust Your promises and Your love. I trust the blood of Jesus that has washed me into new life. Amen.

Strength to Strength

They go from strength to strength.
Psalm 84:7 KJV

You know the strength I need to face today, Lord. You know the strength I'll need for tomorrow, for next week, for next year. You know what I'll need to face each of the challenges that lie ahead in my life. You know the day of my death, and You know exactly what I'll need on that day, too. So I need not worry about anything. You will lead me from strength to strength, like jumping from stone to stone across a river.

What Will Be

The earth will be full of the knowledge
of the Lord as the waters cover the sea.

Isaiah 11:9 nasb

Dear Father, the more I know about Your creation, the more I marvel at the mind that conceived it. The more I marvel at You. Your creation is irreducibly complex, multifaceted, and breathtakingly beautiful whether viewed from a satellite or in a microscope. And we are only just beginning *to begin* to fathom its mysteries. I praise You for the spirit of inquiry that You fashioned in us along with the breath of life. I praise You that You are *knowable*. And I praise You for the day when we will know You fully. Amen.

Coveting

Let your conduct be without covetousness.
HEBREWS 13:5 NKJV

God, it's so easy to break the tenth commandment: do not covet (see Exodus 20:17). Coveting is a way of life for many in our world. But You say we shouldn't compare ourselves with the "Joneses," nor envy them and what they have. Whatever You've given me is to be enjoyed and received, not held up for inspection. Teach me a deeper gratefulness for Your blessings. In Jesus' name, amen.

DAY 332

With Jesus

Father, I will that they also, whom thou hast given me, be with me where I am; that they may behold my glory, which thou hast given me.
JOHN 17:24 KJV

God, as much as I may wish I knew what the future holds, only You know what will happen. Instead of worrying about things that I cannot control, I want to simply follow You into tomorrow and into eternity. The truth is, I don't really care where You lead me. . .so long as Jesus is there, too.

DAY 333

Joy

For ye shall go out with joy, and be led forth with peace: the mountains and the hills shall break forth before you into singing, and all the trees of the field shall clap their hands.
ISAIAH 55:12 KJV

Some days, Lord, things are going so well that it feels like all of creation is singing Your praises, and I join with them. Other days, even when creation sings, I don't feel like praising. Thank You, Lord, for the reminder from the mountains and trees that no matter what today brings, You promise me joy. Help me live out Your joy every day.

I Will Lift Up Mine Eyes

Let the rivers clap their hands,
let the mountains sing together for joy.
PSALM 98:8 NIV

Lord, I praise You for mountains. I praise You for the old, rolling backs of the Appalachians. I praise You for the sharp, unworn spires of the Himalayas. I praise You for snowcapped peaks and glacier-grooved summits and the way mountains train my eyes *upward*. Lord, I so often fix my eyes on the pebbles at my feet, on the trivialities that trip me and dog my path. Give me Your eyes, Lord. Give me the long view. Thank You for this trail I am on, Lord, the sights along the way, and the vista that awaits at the end. Amen.

Let It Be

And Mary said, Behold the handmaid of the Lord;
be it unto me according to thy word.
LUKE 1:38 KJV

Lord, help me follow Mary's example when she
found out that she was pregnant with the Son of
God. Her world was rocked, God! What a scandal!
A good Jewish girl pregnant before she was married? Unthinkable! But she accepted the news and
surrendered her life and her body to Your will.
Help me accept Your Word, no matter what it says
to me, and surrender myself to it.

Right Motives

*Ye ask, and receive not, because ye ask amiss,
that ye may consume it upon your lusts.*

JAMES 4:3 KJV

God, I admit that sometimes I am guilty of treating my prayers as a wish list to a Santa-God. Or maybe I treat You as though You were a vending machine—if I say the right words in the right order, I'll get what I want. If I'm honest, I know that selfishness and greed may slip into a request here or there. Today I ask that You show me when my prayers are corrupted by selfish desires. Give me pure motives, a pure heart, and a clear conscience.

DAY 337

Golden Words Needed

*A word fitly spoken is like apples
of gold in settings of silver.*
PROVERBS 25:11 NKJV

Heavenly Father, today I need affirming words. You know that words are important to me as a woman. You also know that I struggle with self-worth. The other people in my world don't always meet my need to be affirmed verbally, and I can't expect them to fill every void in my life. So, Lord, let me look to and in Your Word to find the love and encouragement I need. In Jesus' name, amen.

Overtaken

But My words and My statutes,
which I commanded My servants the prophets,
did they not overtake and take hold of your
fathers? So they repented.
ZECHARIAH 1:6 AMP

So often, Lord, when I imagine witnessing to someone, I think I have to have every argument and counterargument planned out twelve moves in advance, like it's a chess game. I think of potential questions, and if I don't have perfect answers for them, that's enough to keep me from opening my mouth at all. But Your Word is so clear: *we* do not convert the lost. The Gospel is *alive*. It converts. It overtakes. Lord, I trust Your Word and its mighty power to do what I cannot. Amen.

DAY 339

Confidence

And this is the confidence that we have in him,
that, if we ask any thing according
to his will, he heareth us.

1 JOHN 5:14 KJV

As I pray, Lord, I rest in the confidence that You are always listening and that You understand the thoughts behind my prayers, even when I cannot. I am never speaking into empty air! Thank You for the confidence I also experience through the power of Your Holy Spirit that lives inside my heart. With You on my side, I can accomplish much for Your kingdom!

DAY 340

The Truth

Jesus saith unto him, I am the way, the truth,
and the life: no man cometh unto the Father,
but by me.

JOHN 14:6 KJV

When I pray to You, God, I pray in Your Son's name.
He is the Way, He is the Truth, and He will show
me the way to You so that I can live the life that
You intend for me. Help me to not be distracted
by other false paths that may seem attractive or
easier. Make my journey one that invites others to
follow me, just as I follow Christ.

A Joyful Noise

Shout joyfully to the LORD, all the earth;
break forth in song, rejoice, and sing praises.
PSALM 98:4 NKJV

Dear God, I thank You for music. For the music of rain on rooftops and wind in bare branches. For the splash of water over stones. For little children shouting a hymn at the top of their lungs. For a Bach organ concerto. Lord, Your creation praises You all the time, with every breath and in every moment. Thank You for letting me join in this eternal song of praise. Hallelujah! Worthy is the Lamb who was slain!

United in Prayer

I say unto you, That if two of you shall agree on
earth as touching any thing that they shall ask,
it shall be done for them of my Father
which is in heaven.

MATTHEW 18:19 KJV

Thank You, Lord, for others who share my faith in You. Thank You for the privilege of praying with them, for worshipping with them, for working together to build Your kingdom. Thank You that when we pray together, You hear us and that when we gather together, You are there with us. Help us to be the living, breathing, and active body of Christ that we are meant to be.

Dry Mouth

We also believe and therefore speak.
2 Corinthians 4:13 nkjv

Lord, You can use anyone to spread the good news. You can use invalids, the elderly, fishermen, the mentally challenged, paupers, rich men, tax collectors, children, even me. Thank You that You don't require me to know everything or have every answer. You don't require me to be well traveled or well dressed. You don't require a seminary degree. You don't require me to be anything but saved by the blood of Jesus. The only requirement for evangelism is that I believe and speak. Lord, I believe. Now open my mouth.

Abiding

If ye abide in me, and my words abide in you,
ye shall ask what ye will,
and it shall be done unto you.
JOHN 15:7 KJV

Father, help me abide in You as I pray—not quickly spitting out my requests and then dwelling on my worries and woes. Keep my thoughts focused on You as I wait for Your answers to my prayers, no matter how soon You answer them. Keep me close and allow me to abide in You as You ultimately answer my requests and give me the peace of knowing that You work all things for good.

Wavering Hearts

Let him ask in faith, nothing wavering.
For he that wavereth is like a wave of the sea
driven with the wind and tossed.
JAMES 1:6 KJV

You know how easily my heart wavers and wobbles, Lord. I'm like a boat that's out in open water, the world's woes tossing me around like high waves. Take the helm of my boat, I pray. And then after I've given over control of the boat, quiet the wind and waves. Help me pray with faith's absolute calm, knowing that You have already ordained the outcome and that You have my best interest at heart.

To a God Who Made Giraffes

*Then our mouth was filled with laughter
and our tongue with joyful shouting.*

PSALM 126:2 NASB

Dear Lord, I praise You for laughter. Tonight I laughed until my sides ached, and it was *good*. Now I feel cleansed and emptied of distress and strangely content. Thank You for being a God whose miracles bring laughter: Sarah with the news of her improbable baby, Lazarus raised to life, and the disciples with their ridiculous catch of fish. I can imagine You standing there, Lord, and laughing until the tears came with the people You love. Thank You for giraffes and hedgehogs and zebras and penguins, and how You long to astonish us with joy. Amen.

Poise

Like a gold ring in a pig's snout is a beautiful
woman who shows no discretion.
PROVERBS 11:22 NIV

Heavenly Father, I need poise—that kind of gracious manner and behavior that characterized women of past generations. It seems to be disdained in my culture. Women now are expected and encouraged to be free spirits—unrestricted by convention and decorum. But I cringe when I observe women using crude language, slouching in their seats, and adopting careless ways of walking and eating. I don't want to seem prissy and uppity, but I do want to guard against being too informal. Help me develop the traits that portray womanhood as the gentle, beautiful, fascinating gender You designed. Amen.

Anything!

For verily I say unto you, That whosoever shall say unto this mountain, Be thou removed, and be thou cast into the sea; and shall not doubt in his heart, but shall believe that those things which he saith shall come to pass; he shall have whatsoever he saith.

MARK 11:23 KJV

I don't want to throw any mountains into the ocean, God—and it's hard for me to believe that Jesus really meant what He said here. Show me the truth of His words. Teach me to pray according to Your will.

Power

*The effectual fervent prayer of a
righteous man availeth much.*
JAMES 5:16 KJV

Sometimes I say, "The only thing I can do now is
pray." I mean that I've done everything I could
think to do, and now as a last resort, I'll fall back on
prayer. Forgive me, Father, for trusting in things
that are not from You and for setting my mind on
worldly things. Remind me that prayer is never the
last resort and that You are faithful in hearing it.
Teach me to see the power that prayer can unleash
in the world.

Well Begun Is Half Done

Now faith is the substance of things hoped for,
the evidence of things not seen.
HEBREWS 11:1 NKJV

Dear God, there is something You've asked me to do that I've been putting off for a long time. You haven't forgotten—though *I've* certainly tried to. You keep gently reminding and prodding me to obey. Tonight, as I was walking and pondering this in the darkness between streetlights, I was filled with a cheerful certainty that by the next day, I would have begun. And this wasn't wishful thinking, was it, Lord? It was *faith*. Thank You for believing in what is not yet visible in me and allowing me to do the same. Amen.

Lessons in Trust

I have put my trust in the Lord GOD,
that I may declare all Your works.
PSALM 73:28 NKJV

Heavenly Father, teach me to trust. I know it's an area of weakness for me. In spite of the fact that I know Your character and Your track record, I find it so difficult to relinquish to You the important areas of life. Oh, I say that I will, and I do put forth effort to rely on You, but we both know that, in my heart, I find it hard to let You handle everything. So take my hand, Lord, and teach me to trust. You're the Master; I am forever Your student. In Christ's name, amen.

DAY 352

In All My Ways

In all thy ways acknowledge him,
and he shall direct thy paths.
PROVERBS 3:6 KJV

God, I claim Your presence in each aspect of my life. Thank You for Your steadfast love and abounding grace. I honor You alone with my successes and acknowledge Your guiding hand on my life. Help me set my eyes only on You. Teach me what it is to trust You with all my heart and to not lean on my own wisdom or understanding. May my heart always seek to bring glory to Your name and may my prayers always reflect this reality.

DAY 353

Willing Mind

Know thou the God of thy father, and serve him with a perfect heart and with a willing mind: for the LORD searcheth all hearts, and understandeth all the imaginations of the thoughts: if thou seek him, he will be found of thee.

1 CHRONICLES 28:9 KJV

Make my mind willing, Lord. Help me trust that Your plans for me are better than the plans I have for myself. Place Your desires in my heart, that I may be able to walk fully in Your will for my life. Help me agree with Your ways for my life. I seek You who understands me completely.

The Giver

*You open your hand and satisfy
the desires of every living thing.*
PSALM 145:16 NIV

Lord, I've never been hungry; I've never been naked; I've never been without shelter. You have been a faithful provider of the things You know I need. Thank You for my parents, who provided for me from birth to age twenty-three. And thank You for my husband, who has so faithfully provided for me in the years since then. Thank You, Lord, for providing for me through their generosity and hard work. It's humbling to realize that I've never been completely self-sufficient at any point in my life, yet there is a lesson in that, too. We are paupers by nature: *all* is from You. I praise my open-handed God! Amen.

Perfect Heart

Let your heart therefore be perfect with the LORD our God, to walk in his statutes, and to keep his commandments, as at this day.
1 KINGS 8:61 KJV

You know I can never achieve perfection on my own, Lord God. But I surrender my heart to You absolutely. Keep my heart and mind from wandering and allow me to remain true only to You. I thank You for Your never-ending grace that sustains my life and that You never leave me or forsake me. Through my prayer, I commit myself totally to You and Your law for my life.

Divine Guidance

If any of you lacks wisdom, you should ask God,
who gives generously to all without finding fault,
and it will be given to you.

JAMES 1:5 NIV

Dear Lord, it's so hard sometimes to know what Your will is. You don't write specific instructions in the sky nor emblazon them on a marquee. So how can I know exactly what You want me to do? How can I keep from making a big mistake? How can I proceed with this decision? I ask today that You would give me wisdom, send me guidance as I seek Your will. Through a person, a thought, a scripture, let me sense Your leading for this situation. I want my life to honor Your plan for me. In Christ's name, amen.

Celebration

*They celebrate your abundant goodness and
joyfully sing of your righteousness.*
PSALM 145:7 NIV

Dear Father, so many people who don't know You
see You as a heavenly killjoy: stopping them from
doing really fun things that would bring them great
enjoyment. But we know You better! Thank You
that You do not delight in denial: You delight in
saying yes to Your people. But more importantly,
You delight in *us* and what is for our ultimate good,
not just fun for a moment. And You are planning
the ultimate party—one that will last forever. I
can't wait to join the celebration! Amen.

Willing

*I know also, my God, that thou triest the heart,
and hast pleasure in uprightness. As for me,
in the uprightness of mine heart I have
willingly offered all these things.*
1 CHRONICLES 29:17 KJV

I give You, God, everything I have to offer, willingly and gladly. I know that everything I have You have provided and entrusted to me. Give me a whole heart to follow after You and keep Your commandments. Keep forever in my heart Your purposes and thoughts. Show me anything I am holding back. I want You to have it all.

Deep Surrender

But now, O LORD, You are our Father;
we are the clay, and You our potter;
and all we are the work of Your hand.
ISAIAH 64:8 NKJV

Lord, I need to surrender to You. You've shown me an area of my life that I've been trying to rule. I know You need the keys to every room in my heart, and so here I am, bringing this one to You. *Surrender* means I give You permission to change, clean out, and add things. Waving the white flag isn't really easy, but it's the way to true joy. Thank You for showing me that. Amen.

Truthful Heart

Lord, who shall abide in thy tabernacle? Who shall
dwell in thy holy hill? He that walketh uprightly,
and worketh righteousness, and speaketh
the truth in his heart.
PSALM 15:1–2 KJV

Lord, sometimes I lie to myself. Sometimes I try
to lie to You. But You know me. You know my
thoughts before I think them. Reveal to me Your
truth so that my prayers may be true, righteous,
and upright. Show me how to live a blameless life.

His Work

For the eyes of the Lord are on the righteous and his ears are attentive to their prayer.

1 PETER 3:12 NIV

God, I am amazed that You never tire of listening to me. *I* get tired of listening to me, Lord! The same fears, the same complaints, the same problems, the same confusions—year after year. Yet, even I see progress, and I praise You. I am not who I was, and I know it's all because of You. Thank You for how You continue to work in me: so faithfully, patiently, lovingly. You are the Potter; I am the grateful clay in Your hands. Amen.

DAY 362

One Mind

*That ye may with one mind and one mouth glorify
God, even the Father of our Lord Jesus Christ.*
ROMANS 15:6 KJV

Unite me in prayer with others, Father God. Let
no division come between us as we talk with You.
Give me patience in dealing with people who aren't
exactly like me and can be trying; remind me that
patience will build up Your church. Forgive me for
any gossip or malicious words I've spoken against
my brothers and sisters and give me a heart that
longs for their good. Bring to my mind ways I can
show love that will bring more glory to You.

Believing

Be not faithless, but believing.
JOHN 20:27 KJV

I believe in You, Jesus. I believe in Your power and wisdom and love. I believe that Your atoning work on the cross has washed me of all my unrighteousness and that through it, I stand in perfect righteousness before God. Take my life—all my words and deeds—and use them for Your glory. Teach me to trust You, not requiring proof as Thomas did, but believing You at Your Word alone. Thank You that Your Word is truth and brings life to me and to those around me.

Endurance Required

*Let us run with endurance the race
that is set before us.*

HEBREWS 12:1 NKJV

I'm finding, Lord, that the Christian life is one that requires endurance. It isn't enough to start well. So let me patiently and steadily move down the road to Christlikeness. I know difficulties will come; I've faced some already. It reminds me of the words of the second verse of "Amazing Grace": "Through many dangers, toils, and snares, I have already come. 'Tis grace that brought me safe thus far, and grace will lead me home." In Your name, amen.

The Grand Timeline

He has made everything beautiful in its time.
He has also set eternity in the human heart;
yet no one can fathom what God has
done from beginning to end.
ECCLESIASTES 3:11 NIV

Lord, thank You for the grand story of history, which is really *Your* story. I see exploration, discovery, and war all muddled together, repeating, and leading *where?* But You had the end in mind from the beginning. I know I can trust that You are leading us to an end and to a good place. And I praise You for the amazing grace that has allowed my story to be a small part of the story You are telling. Amen.

OLD TESTAMENT

NEW TESTAMENT